dr. ryce's message of forgiveness and healing through relationships is **simple, straightforword and transforming.** Through his seminars and writings, I have learned the tools to create the most Loving relationships I have ever known in my life. michael's work represents the **most powerful work on the planet.** Bruce Dooley, MD, author of *Perfect Health Forever*, Ft. Lauderdale, FL

That **one worksheet**—the first one has had an **impact on every phase of my life**. Without you I might never have found the solution—**I didn't even see the problem**. Now when a member of this family becomes stressed the others in unison say, "Do a worksheet!" Jimnah Shiyr, Farmer, Ava, MO

I now divide my life into "Before the 40 Day Intensive" and "After the 40 Day Intensive"! What a marvelous experience. WOW! My life shifted totally from these new realities. **My life got joyful!** I never imagined I could feel so good so much of the time! **I no longer feel locked out of life.** Patricia Livingston, Therapist, New York, NY

I do believe, to date, the tapes "Why Is This Happening To Me . . . AGAIN?!" have been **the single-most important workshop/ educational experience** which has contributed to my understanding of myself and the world around me. Thank you. Nancy Doughterty, Writer/Editor, Malvern, PA

There aren't words to express my gratitude. **The Commitment has become a mainstay in our family** and has transformed our marriage into a wonderfully strong, supportive and very freeing relationship. S.K., Fayetteville, AR

Thank you for your "Why Is This Happening To Me . . . AGAIN?!" workshop. After 200 sheets in 40 days, even my sister said I'd changed more in 40 days than 4 years of therapy (not to discount therapy). **This is powerful stuff!** R. P., Austin, TX

One workshop—my life has transformed. S.C., Miami, FL

*This 40 Day Intensive has been one of the greatest and most rewarding times of my entire life. **Not only did I do some great work but I had fun. Good simple fun.** I have felt so supported, loved and nurtured by all... I can't begin to tell you how grateful I am and how much your workshops, tapes and the Commitment have started to really create some empowering changes in my life.* Dorrie Evans, Executive, Ft. Lauderdale, FL

*"Why Is This Happening To Me . . . AGAIN?!" is life changing information! **As a therapist I am recommending it to all of my clients.** It has become a valuable tool in the healing of many people in my life already.* Sandra Callahan, Therapist, Conyers, GA

*"Why Is This Happening To Me . . . AGAIN?!" clearly, and irrefutably demonstrates a causal connection for improper thoughts and intentions with mal-adaptive behavior and poor health. **Your treatment of the forgiveness dynamic to correct improper thoughts and intentions is among the best in many centuries.** Your work is a light guiding our way out of pressing social and spiritual difficulties. You have developed a psychology of good, and **it works!*** D. M., Attorney, Albany, GA

***I am amazed at the power** the Reality Management Worksheets have unleashed in my life.* R. R., Austin, TX

***Thanks to your teaching my dad lived.** If we did not have the knowledge, he would have died.* E. J., Misala, Japan

*After 6 months of your work, **business increased 75%... less stress... I feel more capable.*** R.P., Chiropractor, Boca Raton, FL

*The response of both my staff and clients is remarkable. They are saying **'For the first time, I feel hope,'** and your teachings are helping me make **significant changes** in my own life!* P.C., PhD., Comm. Mental Health, W. Palm Beach, FL

WHY IS THIS HAPPENING TO ME . . . AGAIN?!

... AND WHAT YOU CAN DO ABOUT IT

dr. michael ryce

First Edition

First Printing June 1996

ISBN 1-886562-29-6

*This book is in a special binding that allows it to lay flat when
opened and stay together if it is folded back on itself.*

For a free electronic download of
this text, our home page address is:
http:/www.kcmo.com/whyagain

Published by
dr. michael ryce
c/o Rt. 3 Box 3280
Theodosia, Missouri 65761
417-273-4838
whyagain@kcmo.com

This book is dedicated to:

marijo
A Healed Humanity
Our Future Generations
My Parents, Michael and Jessie
My Siblings, Terry, Dorothy Ann, and Alice
My Children, Michael Jay and Christa Joy
Each of You for your willingness to take this journey

This work is committed to:

The restoration of Total Love to every mind
and relationship on the planet

INTRODUCTION

by James Redfield

author of *The Celestine Prophecy*

and *The Tenth Insight*

I first heard of michael ryce's work in 1988. He was speaking in Birmingham, Alabama and, while I was unaware of his lecture at the time, I felt an unusual urge to drive to its location that day. Over and over, the intuition penetrated my awareness, and just as many times I told myself that I was too busy. I had planned to work all day at my desk and I resisted changing my agenda.

Still, the image kept coming to mind. Repeatedly, I saw myself getting up and going there. Finally, after hours of procrastination, I did just that. When I arrived, the lecture was over and michael had left, but enough people remained to let me know what I had missed.

"The breadth of this guy's knowledge is amazing," one person told me. "He brings a new and original understanding of relationship dynamics, he talks about the translations of ancient Aramaic texts, the findings of modern physics, and pulls them all together in a way that makes sense. You missed it, but you're in luck, he has several workshop tapes. It's all there."

Later, I searched out these tapes and found one of his titles— *Why Is This Happening To Me . . . AGAIN?!*—staring down at me from a shelf in a local bookstore. When I got them home, I found that listening to his tapes was to take an amazing journey through the world of inner healing and through michael ryce's mind.

My friends were right. The gift michael has is to synthesize the many diverse elements of the human experience and bring them together into a clear picture of human growth in the world, especially the growth that comes about as the result of the relationships we encounter with other human beings.

His foundation is so diversified it is hard to pin down its exact source. He holds that everyone who comes into our lives is there to teach us something. And he buttresses this foundation by synthesizing the original meanings of the Aramaic Scriptures and the new world view presented by modern physics, which indicates that the force of our intention goes out and influences the world. He emphasizes the understanding that this influence is not restricted just to conscious thought, but applies to the unconscious state of mind as well. In other words, the way we think about the world and the unconscious attitudes we harbor, to a great degree influence what happens to us in life.

That's why the title of his tape series, and this book you are about to read, is so poignant and totally on target. *"Why Is This Happening To Me . . . AGAIN?!"* is what all of us feel at one time or another if we are open and honest. We feel this way because our unconscious habits of mind keep bringing the same types of people and events into our lives repeatedly, and will continue to do so until we change the mental patterns that attract such outcomes.

What michael is doing is offering a coherent system for change by which we can remove the self-defeating obstacles that block our way and open up to the real path that awaits us in life. It's a journey of clearing that each of us must take, sooner or later. Of the approaches I've seen on how our thoughts and habits affect what happens to us, michael ryce's work is the most succinct and helpful at opening us to growth. If you're like I was, thinking you don't have time, pause a moment and take a tip from me: exploration into your inner beliefs and expectations through michael's work, right now . . . can shift your life forever.

Thanks, michael, for the inspiration all these years!

James Redfield

ACKNOWLEDGMENTS

Deep appreciation and Love to you, **marijo**, for your monumental support in making this book happen and joining with me in healing ourselves, each other and the planet. *I Love you!*

From the bottom of my heart, I thank you, **William Corley,** for all of your patience, enthusiasm, management skills, computer knowledge, and the long hours spent on this book.

A special eternal thanks and Love to **Angie Nerber**!

This work did not source from its author. It is a synthesis of the interaction, ideas, and Love of many wonderful people who have been my teachers and my support system. Deep gratitude and thanks for your caring, you are in my heart for eternity! This list by no means covers everyone who deserves thanks for their part in this work and is intended to offer a taste of the scope and variety of people who have helped to shape what you are about to read.

Gloria Abbott and Travis and William Corley, Joy Adams, Jon and Lisa Addiss, Ruth Addiss and "Clint," Dr. John and Sandy Affleck, Gloria and Bob Albu, Terry and Sasha Alexandra, Christian Almayrac, Arden Anderson, John and Norma Anderson, Dr. Seneca and Kay Anderson, Janis and Jerry Aurillo & family, Dick and Marylee Bacharach & family, W. H. and Linda Baker, Jerry and Jane Barthalow, Mary Bauer, Rex and Mitzi Bauer & family, Dr. Bob Beck, Ray and Marilyn Bekiaris & family, Bill and Mary Jane Belfie, Claudio Belfort, Dave Bent, Katheryn Bernhardt, Glen Berquist & family, Dick and Francesca Bertram, Jamie Black, Judith Blommel, Bob and Sara Bochek & family, Carol Boggs, Mary and Haven Boggs, Tony Bonaccorso, Ken and Ruth Borders, Dr. Paul Bragg and Patricia, Jodale Brodnax, John Brook, Ed Brouwers.

Sandra and Dan Callahan, Diana Campbell, Maria Carr, Ron and Roberta Carson, Elaine Casey, Chris Chenoweth, Patricia Clayson, Ros Corson, Jeanne Copeland, Ted and Lucy Cowan & family, Jan Cox, Charles Crawford & family, Patsy and Sara Crawford, Bruce Cummings, Bill Curry, Don and Kathy Curry & family, Richard and Diana Daffner, Dianne Dalton, Mike and Coleen DeCrecente, Nick Dejnega, Durk DeJong, Carol O'Connel and Don Dicenza, Dr. Jay Dishman, Dean and Vera Dixon, Pat and Irene Doody,

Dr. Bruce Dooley, Dr. Larry Dossey, Nancy Dougherty, Ginger Duke, Boone and Susan Dunlap, Dr. Gary Dunlap, Judy and Walter Dunn & family, David Durovey, Dennis Duvale, Wilberta and Richard Eastman & family, Barb Edwards, Ron Edwards, Claudia Ellard, Cathrine El Mandeau, Dr. Rocco Erico, Dorrie Evans.

Ruth Fannin, Jim and Marcia Farmer & family, Gil Fatheringham, Bob Fatheringham, Paul Ferrini, Lynn Fisher and La Wanda Shellan, Marjorie Freed, Charles and Myrtle Filmore, Thurman Fleet, Loren and Crissy Flickenger, Dr. Sharon Forest, Robert, Jerry and Tess Fridenstine & family, Willard Fuller, Margaret Fuller-Hiller, Roberta Furtell, Edwene and Burt Gaines, Mahatma Gandhi, Michael and Janet Gerrace, Graeme Gibson and Gail Simmons, Connie Glass, Joel and Betty Goldstein & family, George and Jackie Gordon & family, Dr. Thomas Gorman, James Goure, Jonathon Goure, Linda Graham, Ali Guggenheim.

Steve Halpern, Jim Hargett, Trudy Harris, Kim and Julie Haverstick, Dr. Doug Hays, Dave and Alice Henderson & family, Joanne Himes, Jim and Vonny Heinecamp, Faye Heinecamp, Carol Hess, Jim Hodnett, Dale Hoffman, Ernest Holmes, Fr. Keith Hosey, Ken and Janet Houdon-Jorgenson, Bunton and Angie Humphry & family, Charlotte and Dr. Conway Hunter, Jennifer Hurley, William and Jay Irman.

Michael and Jayne James & family, Dr. Bernard Jensen, Dee Jenson, Betty and Martha Johnson, Chick and Gloria Johnson, Elaine and Leighton Johnson & family, Amral Kahn & family, Pirjo Kaikkonen & family, Judge Asa Kelly, Ruth Kenyon and Brian, Don and Gena Key & family, Jade Khalsa, Bill King, Lou Kircher, Dr. Robert Knapp, Ava Knickle, Dr. James and Gail Krumholtz & family, Penny Kubitschek, Viktoras Kulvinskas, Mary and Bill Kupferle, Kath Kvols and Brian, Ken and Sheila Ladd & family, Dr. George Lamsa, Phil Laut, Dr. Louis Leonardi, Betty and Jerry Leunig, Sam Levy, Bill and Dorthy Leyland, Loretta Lines, Dr. Edward and Ruth Lindwall, Terry Livingood, Drs. Robert and Cecile Locke, Herb and Gail Long, Kevin and Dorothy Ann Loosemore & family, Dr. Ed Luddeke, Daniel and JJ Lyman & family.

Dan and June MacDougald, Drs. Lenny and Nelly Macheret & family, Sr. Maureen Mangen, Lori and Michael Martin/Redhair & family, Glen Massnick, Sandy Maurer, Debi and Kevin McGuire & family, R. A. McMaster, Diane Maun, Shawn and Zmenz McCarty & family, Joan McClure, Sue and Leo McDonald, Patrick McGhan & family, Dr. William J. McKenzie, Howard and Norma McPherson & family, Donna Maas, James and Salle Merril-Redfield, Dr. Steve and Brenda Meyerson, Drs. Brian and Light Miller, Dr. Steven Miller, Sam Mirshak and Flora, George Morey, Glen Mosley, Father Sean Mucahey, Jeff Mueller, Ryan Mueller, Lisa Jean Mullen, Eileen and Harold Murphy & family, Clyde Nessler, Mary Ann Oertel, Frank Oddo, Oman and Shante, Leonard Orr, Dr. John Ott.

Brook Pablo, Baine Palmer, Pat Palmer, Steve and Judy Paskoski & family, Dr. David and Michelle Pesek, Dr. Wayne and Lori Pharr & family, Judy and Bill Phelan, Wayne Pickering, Robert and Marietta Pickett, Dr. Richard Plagenhoef, Glen Powell, Dr. Carl Pribram, Henry Pringer, Steve Procko, Jean Rampage, Elinor Ray, John Ray, Dr. John Ray, Bill Reidler, John and Donna Rietschlin & family, Penny Ripple, Jeanne Rindge, Bengt Robbert, Dr. Dan Roehm, Michael Rose, Mary Rossini, Dr. Larry Reuter, Dr. Leo Roy, Honey Ruben, Rukha and family, C. J. (Carol) Ryce, Edward and Alice Ryce & family, Michael Jay and Christa Joy Ryce, Terry and Pat Ryce and family, Tommy Ryce & family, Kermit Rydell, Sally Rydell.

Paula Sabo, Marguerite Scheffler, Scot Scheffler, Phil and Willa Schlegel, Helen Schucman, Shay St. John and Al Sears, Geri and Bill Senn, Dr. Greg and Margarette Sharpe & family, Susan Shaw, Jerry De Shazo, Jimnah and Diana Shiyr, Stu and Sandy Shmitt, Ruby Skellen, Jim and Ella Skene, James and Margaret Skene & family, Vic Skene, Robert and Judith Skutch, Fran, Chester and Curtis Sliwa, Gary Smith, Dr. Leonard and Jane Smith, Larry Snyder, Joya Spalding & family, Dr. Ginny St. Clare, Joe St. Pierre, Dr. Edith Stauffer, Brenda and Stavi Starchild, Liz Sterling, Norm Stewart, Barbara & Joey Stevens, Robert Stevens, Michael Stillwater, Kathleen Stone, Dean Stonier, Mary Stradley, Peter Strinno & family, Dr. John Sundquist, Howard Swadron, Gloria Schwemley, Robert Schwemley, Dr. Gordon Swensen, Peggy and Ferenc Szony & family.

Joyce and Teressa Tasone, Bill Thedford, Alex Thomas, Donna Thomas, Debbie Thomarios, Tom Thorpe, Sandra Tillman, Fran and Lori Tiner & family, Toni Toney, Ron Toplin, Bud and Pauline Totten, Dr. "Barefoot" Fred and Meredith Troxel & family, Debby Tyson, Dr. John Upledger, Richard Utt, Lenny Valencourt, Nina Vance, Dr. Randolf Vance, Doug Bingley and Kathy Veith, James Van Eyck, Marcel Vogel, John Waldon, Dr. Norman Walker, Dr. Charles Warth, Linda and Jim Washington, Dr. Curtis and Marilyn Watson & family, Bob Watts, Bill Weeks, Phillis Weis, Richard and Donna Welch, John and Louise Weldon and family, Rod and Ann Wells & family, Carol Westwood, Dr. Robert and Charolotte Wicker-Shaw, Dr. Ann Wigmore, Maurice Williams, Robert Williamson & family, Tim Willis, Mary Ann Wise, B. J. Woodyard, Alce Wyatt, Phil Zimmerman.

Appreciation to all of you, known and unknown, who have contributed to and supported this work.

CONTENTS

IS THIS BOOK FOR YOU?
An Overview by the Author

Have you ever had conflict in your relationships? Attempted the geographic cure? Tried unsuccessfully to change others?

Have you had thoughts like: *"Why Is This Happening To Me . . . AGAIN?!* Why are they doing this to me... again?! Why am I doing this to myself... again?! Why can't life just cooperate?!"

This book presents practical tools for change. People who participate in our workshops report significantly improved relationships, creativity, finances and eating habits. Many say their health and energy levels are better and that their mental functions and emotional stability are enhanced. We are told that victimhood and addictions drop away, spiritual health increases, and peace of mind becomes their normal and natural state.

Please read the book for an overview before focusing on its subtle points. It takes time to *build the brain cells* for significant change to take place and to understand some of the ideas that will be presented in this work. Brain cells are the body's storage system for information and **"Building Brain Cells"** refers not to building physical structure but to storing information for future recall. Using the suggested tools will fill in the blanks and open the far-reaching implications of this work.

Like any new language, this material may be confusing at first—it might be all Greek to you. A learning curve is normal with any new information. Unraveling old patterns and teaching your mind new ways to function takes time. Beware the tendency of the mind to reject what is inconsistent with your current beliefs. I suggest that you set aside anything that does not fit your thinking and see how those pieces work as you "build" new information into brain cells. Invest the time and you will be amazed at what you will comprehend from these pages. After intense interaction it will feel as if a mental switch is thrown and understanding falls into place.

To reap endless benefits from this work does not require belief, understanding or agreement! The skeptic who dares to simply put the pen to the paper and actually uses these tools will produce dramatic life-changing results!

THE CHALLENGE OF LIFE CONSISTS NOT IN EXPLORING

NEW LANDSCAPES BUT IN DEVELOPING NEW EYES.

Marcel Proust 1871-1922

As a result of completing this text, the reality structure in your mind will change; *life will be seen with new eyes!* This book will seem to change but, of course, it remains the same. Your perception of this material and of the world will shift as new levels of application and meaning unfold.

This book is designed to be a source of clarity and empowerment now and in the future. To receive full benefit from its design, customize this book by writing in it. Please:

Write   Scribble   **EXPRESS YOURSELF**

THINK   *GET MESSY*   Be Elegant

CONTEMPLATE   CREATE   FABRICATE   **REASON**

ANALYZE   *Compose*   DRAW   PLAY

Love   **REFLECT**   gEt cRAzY   Get Sane!

Surprisingly, as you use these tools, aspects of life that once seemed miserable will become enjoyable! For instance, if you have a pattern where it seems you have no choices in life, *use* of the tools transforms those times into an empowering opportunity to learn choice. For some, their rage, grief or fear seems uncontrollable. With tools, surfacing the uncontrollable becomes an opportunity to gain freedom and to develop joy, strength, and aliveness through the healing of destructive emotions!

You may find yourself yelling at or arguing with this book (or me—please be gentle!). Talk or scream if necessary! It can be an important step into sanity. This manual is designed to bring up and support the healing of any energy in you that undermines aliveness. During this process you will encounter everything in your mind, including enormous Love!

Richard represents a composite of a thousand conversations with *real* people. Any resemblance to people you know, is purely intentional and highly probable. If he triggers issues or feelings in you that you would prefer to avoid—great! Be aware that your healing journey is about to take another step. If you identify with him, this text offers you ample space to look at yourself. Beware the tendency to think that he, or words on a page, could possibly be responsible for *anything* you feel; however, he may give you some opportunities to heal!

The dialogue between michael and the troubled Richard is fast paced, nurturing and enlightening. You will be gripped by the way he unravels the blocks that keep him from receiving the Love for which he yearns. You will cheer as he rebuilds his understanding of the dynamics of his life, his confused childhood, and his muddled, seemingly hopeless relationships. You will join him in learning step-by-step tools that will enhance your life—and you don't need to be in turmoil or upset for life to get better! People from all over the world, including those who have created wonderful lives for themselves, have benefited from refining their life skills by using these tools.

This process requires courage and will not always be "Dr. Feelgood," however, the rewards and results will impact you and your family in wonderful and beautiful ways—for eternity.

Blessings, Love and support on your journey!

michael

author's notes

This body of work presents tools which can be used to manage your mind, *body*, relationships and life. The first decades of my life, I lived without them. Approximately 25 years ago, as a result of the need to heal myself, I searched for tools with which I could unload the burdens I had accumulated. This book is one of the results of that search. This work is not a product of any curriculum. It is written from my own experience and is offered with sincere humility. I know of no book from which inner work can be learned, though thousands of books have been written about it. Acquiring this knowledge is a process.

None of what appears on these pages is original, save the synthesis of the material and some of the conclusions, for which I take full responsibility and invite your input. Nothing herein should be construed as medical advice as each idea is intended for support of the reader's Spiritual process and *self*-healing.

Using these tools calls for a different mind-set than the all too common "victim" or "hero" attitude and requires time, work and willingness. The tools work; the rewards are extraordinary! Take the time to build the foundation and understand the philosophy of this work, and you will create a toolbox which makes these *Tools For Life* usable. Your life is about to change.

This book covers both the introductory course material and the advanced material, designed for those more involved. This material flows from a course of study which now takes a minimum of nine days to complete at our teaching center. In my short, two-and-one-half hour workshops, I invite people to "listen fast." The amount of material covered in this book is enormous and rarely would it be possible to comprehend it all in one reading. To you, the reader, I suggest, digest slowly. *Be patient.* Ten years from now, on the twentieth or ninetieth reading, due to the nature of this work, this book will say many new things to you.

I suggest you read as much of the text as makes sense to you and *do* the worksheet process. If you lose the train of thought or confusion surfaces, go back and *do* the worksheet. This book is not meant to be grasped in one reading.

Many people find that a combination of the written course material and the audio or video tapes helps them grasp this information more quickly. I realize this may sound a bit like a commercial, but we've found that exposing people to this work through as many different senses as possible helps them integrate it and put the tools to use more quickly. When you see this workshop on video or hear it on cassette tape, it is almost as though it produces a three-dimensional or cellular comprehension. It is a difficult effect to explain and even more difficult to achieve through a linear presentation such as happens with written material.

The goal of this text is to create a theoretical framework from which to view life differently. Above all, I wish to stress the simplicity of the process you are about to engage in, though it may appear complex at first. Truth is complex to a complex mind and simple to a simplified mind.

I understand that scientific convention and the rational mind require that I cite references for each new statement. I have chosen to bypass convention. I will make many statements that are based solely on my observations after twenty-five years of doing this work. I invite you to disbelieve everything I say and test it for yourself. Verification will come from the fact that you will find the tools work. I invite correction and feedback on this material and present what I consider to be useful observations even though they do not fit convention. I am in agreement with Albert Einstein who said: *"One thing I have learned in a long life: that all our science, measured against reality, [actuality] is primitive and childlike."*

The scientific method provides a platform, as it were, from which to view the world. Any theory breaks down where its foundation is flawed and becomes provable from within its own errors. There was a time when everyone "knew" the world was flat;

thousands died of scurvy years after nutritional deficiency was known to be at least part of that dis-ease and limes were proposed as a solution; the first physician to suggest that medicine men spread disease with dirty hands was scorned as a fool. Many so called "scientific" minds resist change. Scientific conventions seem to change only when those with old beliefs die.

You will hear a lot about the Law of Love in this book. It is the guardrail on the highway of reason. Information available to a mind is limited by the mind-set of the "thinker." Do you see all the things you Love about a person when anger rears its head? No, we are cut off from our Loving thoughts by anger, cut off from the Law of Love.

The intellect, because of the way our mind-set limits available information, can "logically" take you anywhere its foundation is set to go; it can justify anything up to and including murder. Love, as a condition in the mind, inoculates the intellect against foolish and senseless behavior. A lack of awareness of the Law of Love is *the recipe* for insanity because without it the mind must operate under the rules that produce insanity. The Law of Love is the *only* pathway to peace of mind which is a prerequisite to sanity and happiness.

The goal of this work is summed up in the story of a child of four who had shown an interest in geography. One day her mother cut up a map of the world to make a puzzle, thinking it would keep the little girl busy for a few days. Fifteen minutes after receiving the map, the little girl had assembled the puzzle. Her mother was shocked, she couldn't believe it. "How did you put the puzzle together so quickly? Even I couldn't have done that."

The girl replied, "Well, Mom, I noticed when you were cutting out the map of the world, there was a picture of a little girl on the other side. When I put the little girl together, the whole world came together!"

ENJOY!

THE DILEMMA

The mass of men lead lives of quiet desperation.
What is called resignation is confirmed desperation.
From the desperate city you go into the desperate country
and have to console yourself with the bravery of minks and
muskrats. A stereotyped but unconscious despair is
concealed even under what are called the games and
amusements of mankind. To be awake is to be alive.
I never yet met a man who is quite awake.

Henry David Thoreau

THE SOLUTION

If you advance confidently in the direction of your dreams,
and endeavor to live the life you have imagined, you will meet
with the success unexpected in common hours. You will pass
an invisible boundary... If you have built castles in the air,
your work need not be lost; that is where they should be.
Now put the foundation under them.

Henry David Thoreau

LIFE WITH TOOLS IS AWAKENING AND DELIGHT.
INFORMATION WITH TOOLS IS POWER.
POWER WITH TOOLS IS SERVICE.
RELATIONSHIP WITH TOOLS IS INTER-DEPENDENCE.
KNOWLEDGE WITH TOOLS IS SAFETY.
COMMITMENT WITH TOOLS IS A BLESSING.
ABUNDANCE WITH TOOLS IS EASY.
HEALTH WITH TOOLS IS NATURAL.
LEARNING WITH TOOLS IS EDUCATION.
AMBITION WITH TOOLS IS ACCOMPLISHMENT.
A WORLD WITH TOOLS IS PEACEFUL.
HAVING TOOLS AND *USING* THEM LEADS TO ALIVENESS.

LIFE WITHOUT TOOLS IS SLEEP AND HELL.
INFORMATION WITHOUT TOOLS IS IMPOTENCE.
POWER WITHOUT TOOLS IS DICTATORSHIP.
RELATIONSHIP WITHOUT TOOLS IS CO-DEPENDENCE.
KNOWLEDGE WITHOUT TOOLS IS DANGEROUS.
COMMITMENT WITHOUT TOOLS IS HOPELESS.
ABUNDANCE WITHOUT TOOLS IS LOSS.
HEALTH WITHOUT TOOLS IS IMPOSSIBLE.
LEARNING WITHOUT TOOLS IS CHAOS.
AMBITION WITHOUT TOOLS IS CORRUPTION.
A WORLD WITHOUT TOOLS IS WAR.
HAVING TOOLS AND *NOT USING* THEM IS LIFE WITHOUT TOOLS.

1

THE DILEMMA

Richard, a successful man in his late thirties, was on his way out West following the breakup of another marriage when he called early one morning. "I just finished reading the book, *The Celestine Prophesy* by James Redfield. The friend who gave it to me told me about your work and suggested I give you a call when I got to Springfield. He said you might have some answers for me and help me make sense of things. I don't know, maybe it's a waste of time for us to meet, but my life is a mess... and I'm desperate."

Springfield is an hour-and-a-half drive northwest of *Heartland*, where we do our intensive workshops. I had a few days between finishing our summer season and leaving to go on tour, so I invited Richard to meet with me later that morning. He agreed.

It was a clear, crisp day and the leaves were taking on fall colors. As I watched him climb from his car, Richard appeared taller than I had imagined. He was wearing jeans and a navy blazer over a faded blue tee-shirt, and running shoes instead of the mountain boots I had expected for someone traveling to the West. He appeared as if he could fit in anywhere and be at home with almost anyone. His face showed intelligence and sensitivity, but carried obvious traces of sadness; the slump of his shoulders indicated what appeared to be sizable emotional burdens.

His tales of broken relationships and marriages started before we had even settled into the house. Typical of many of us before we finally look for alternatives to the way we've been taught to live,

Richard expressed frustration, anger and fear. He seemed to flounder in his pain, using words I have come to know are born in the abuse we visit upon ourselves and others when we blame them.

There was an uncertainty in his voice and what seemed to be a controlled anger bordering on violence. I interpreted this to be a product of tremendous frustration and feeling out of control, issues I encounter often among the individuals with whom I work.

> ⚷ KEY THOUGHT—Violence is an attempt to control. The more insecure or out of control people feel, the more violent will be their speech and actions.

He finished his story and lamented, "Sometimes I feel so hopeless, I wonder if there really are any answers." He looked at me now, deep in his pain, waiting for a response.

"Sounds like things are pretty tough for you right now," I began. "How about taking a deep breath and just being still for a moment? Fortunately, these things pass. We have some powerful tools to assist in speeding up the process and assuring a future that unfolds more easily and peacefully. Has anything like this ever happened to you before? Have you ever felt any of these feelings previously?"

Richard admitted that many times he had experienced these same feelings of rage, and he went on to describe the circumstances surrounding several relationships that had ended abruptly. He related his belief that no matter what he did or how he acted, relationships and life were hopeless. He explained that he was moving again to escape painful memories that haunted him in each city that had been his home. Clearly, he felt victimized, alone and confused about how his life was going.

His dilemma was not knowing what to do; he was afraid of repeating his mistakes. This prevented him from making real choices. Yet, he was defensive about his past having anything to do with the present. He made it perfectly clear that he wanted only to talk about what was going on in his life now, not something that happened years earlier.

"I suggest you notice, Richard, that each 'situation' in your life has one thing in common; *every time 'it' happens, you are there!* **You are the common factor. You play a part, consciously or unconsciously, in every event in your life."**

"Are you telling me I wanted those things to happen to me?" Richard sputtered.

"Wanted, no! Participated in, yes! When you can see and take responsibility for your part in events, things will change. Responsibility is not a weight to carry, but a key to reclaiming your power."

"R-i-g-h-t!" he shot back, crossing his arms as he spoke. "So, everything is my fault and if I just accept blame, and admit that I'm guilty, then everything will be fine. Is that your point? I'm not to blame! If you want to blame somebody, blame them! I've been the victim too many times, and I'm not going to let it happen again!" His teeth were clenched and his shoulders rigid as he glared at me through unblinking eyes.

"If his mind is as closed as his *body* language suggests, my work is definitely cut out for me," I thought. "Looks like maybe you are closing up, Richard. Take a breath; I'm here to support you. My words were 'take responsibility,' not 'you are to blame!' This work is about releasing guilt and blame by seeing *our own* patterns and then healing what is in us that sets up those patterns. My goal is to assist you in recognizing, dealing responsibly with and undoing your part in each painful situation in your life, and learning how to do things differently!

"Blame is an escape from responsibility and a way to give away your power. If what happens in your life is everybody else's fault, then why is it you are the one who has been there every time?" I asked as gently as I could.

The issue that had Richard feeling so much pain was his *Why Is This Happening To Me . . . AGAIN?!* question, which so many of us ask repeatedly as we go through life. It does not matter what the actual event in the outside world is; it could be any combination of relationship issues, employment problems, financial difficulties, or any number of other possibilities. No matter what the circumstances, there is always one common factor: The person having the experience is always involved!

> ☞ KEY THOUGHT—Blame is a way to give away your power and pretend someone else is at fault.

2

WHAT CAUSES OUR PAIN?

Pain, like all feelings, is under the control of the person experiencing it. However, if we refuse responsibility, it will seem that others inflict our pain upon us, and that it is, therefore, inescapable. The pain Richard was experiencing was the result of an internal process; it was not caused by others. In order for Richard to heal, it was essential that he step apart from his *internal dialogue* that convinced him that everyone else was the problem in his life. He had to let go long enough to hear something other than what was going on in his head.

"I hear you saying that you have had many unhappy experiences in your relationships and I understand that your mind makes it look like the source of your pain is outside of you. To think the cause is external is confusing the trigger for your pain with the mechanism that delivers it. The pain you feel is not dependent upon outside events and no one but you can create what you feel inside."

His response was sharp and cutting, "You're just handing me more guilt!" he shot back quickly, "and all I want now is to make sure that what I've been going through doesn't happen again!"

When I introduced Richard to the idea that we are each responsible for our pain, he heard, as many of us do when someone points out that we may have erred, something different. I spoke of responsibility, but Richard interpreted my words to mean other than what I intended. This brought to light an essential element in the healing process. There is a difference between what happens in the world and the mind's interpretation of those events. *One triggers feelings; the other causes them.* Grasping this concept is a key to personal empowerment and the release of pain. What Richard perceived as the "cause" of his unhappiness was nothing more than a trigger which served to bring to awareness an experience stored within him, one which he had repeated so often it was now old and familiar.

"Richard, if you want to create your life differently, you must live from a place of knowing that you are the root cause of all that you experience. Knowing that you are at cause in your life, rather than continuously being triggered into old patterns, is the source of empowerment."

The thought that we are responsible for our lives can be difficult the first time we hear it. Richard appeared to flip-flop between his hunger for understanding and his resistance to taking responsibility.

"For instance, Richard, a few minutes ago I spoke to you of responsibility. What you heard was guilt, fault and blame. As you listened to your internal dialogue, it informed you of the potential pain inherent in being to blame. Next came the defenses you have built up against being at fault and guilty, which are your mind's *interpretation* of responsiblility.

"The reason you don't escape your pain when you leave town or a relationship is that pain is internal and you take it with you when you go. The fact that you can hide your pain successfully does not mean it is gone. There is a toll for hanging on to a negative energy, even when it is not being consciously experienced. Anyone who just says the right words can *trigger* what you are trying to hide from yourself. Your pain is *caused* by the energy you are holding, not by *them*."

> ⚷ KEY THOUGHT—Just because you leave doesn't mean you're not in the same place.

"I don't get this cause and trigger stuff," he prodded.

"Let's see if an example will help to make sense of that," I suggested. "Imagine we place a person from the jungle beside a river and ask him to figure out what causes a drawbridge to open. He observes, time after time, that the bridge goes up when a boat arrives. He further notes that when the boat passes, the bridge lowers. Our observer, not being familiar with bridges, comes to the obvious conclusion that boats cause bridges to go up!

"*We* know that boats can't cause bridges to move either up or down, though they are the trigger that begins the process. Being familiar with bridges, we know that the bridge tender sees a boat and puts the bridge's internal mechanism into motion with the flip of a switch. The switch delivers power to a motor that in turn causes the bridge to go up.

"What if we assign our observer the job of making sure the drawbridge remains down forever? If he clings to the false idea that boats cause bridges to go up, he certainly has his work cut out for him. To accomplish his goal, he may have to change the direction of every boat that approaches, potentially every boat in the world. If, on the other hand, he understands that there is an internal mechanism lifting the bridge, he only needs to get inside the control room and clip one wire and the bridge will remain forever still."

"I see what you mean, michael, and forgive my being blunt," Richard said, "but so what?"

"Richard, this concept is a major key. Your reality arises from inside you. My words are just a trigger for what shows up in your mind. The word 'responsibility' does not include guilt, fault and blame, though that is what you heard. **You must choose to take responsibility for your feelings and what goes on**

inside of you, if you are ever going to change the patterns in your life and heal!"

> ⚷ KEY THOUGHT—If you keep thinking what you've always thought, you'll keep getting what you've always got.

My intention was to assist Richard in seeing that we all have a system of beliefs and ideas which is at the root of our reality structure. Most people talk to themselves all the time, yet remain totally unaware that they are engaged in an inner dialogue which both reviews and reinforces their beliefs about life. Some people are continuously figuring out how to justify themselves in that review, before an inner judge made up of their parents, spouses and any number of other people. "What would the judge say if he saw me doing this?" they ask themselves.

Our internally generated realities and the nature of our continuous silent dialogue operate consistently and automatically in forming the basis of our decisions in life, even the seemingly unimportant or trivial.

I demonstrated the presence of Richard's internal dialogue using the example of his reaction to the word "responsibility." He was unaware that the ideas of guilt, fault and blame came from his self-talk, his own silent speech. More importantly, it had never occurred to him that his perception of reality did not necessarily match the reality shared by the others in his life.

"Richard, our decisions in life arise from our internal reality and contribute to both creating events in our lives *and* generating our feelings about these events. To a great extent, people go through life oblivious to the impact these inner beliefs and ideas have on what happens." I invited Richard to look into the concept that our inner realities and self-talk are governing forces behind the life experiences we create. I suggested he examine his silent dialogue to determine its thrust.

"Many people have lives that include circumstances vastly different from what they would consciously choose. It frequently happens that an individual's self-talk and external talk are focused on what they do *not* want, and so they create their experiences out of avoidance. **Avoidance makes an issue the number one priority in your mind because it focuses your energy on whatever you are avoiding.**"

Richard appeared to be reaching a level of comfort. He leaned forward, resting his elbows on his knees, and was listening intently when a smile floated across his face. "You mean I'm not the only one who talks to himself all the time?"

"No, you are not alone. You can become more aware and take charge of your internal processes if you so choose. Correcting what happens on the inside is the key to creating changes on the outside. **Until you take charge of your internal reality structure, you are bound to keep re-experiencing whatever you are trying to avoid.**"

> ⊙═╦ KEY THOUGHT—Thoughts are how we ask. A thought about what you don't want is as powerful as a thought about what you do want. Be careful what you ask for.

"How do I create the changes I want?" Richard asked.

"The first step is to correct your internal dynamics. I would suggest you change your thoughts about new ideas and let go of the chatter in your head that keeps you from hearing them. It is safe and healing to hear new ideas, and by doing your inner work you will change some of the core interactions you have with life.

"The next step in the process of changing your internal reality is to be responsible for your self-talk. If it doesn't change, then experiences keyed to your old thoughts will keep repeating."

Richard's admission that many times he had experienced the anger he was currently feeling was an indication that his self-talk was helping him repeatedly re-create some of the same realities in his life. "By changing your internal dialogue, your reality structure will change and so will what you attract into your life."

"Sounds like you're saying that in order to change the output, I have to change the focus *and* the input!"

"You've got it, Richard! Everyone knows that in order to change the output of a system, the input needs to change. It does not seem to be common knowledge, however, that in order to change the input of the human system the focus needs to change. **You change your focus by changing your self-talk *and* where you put your attention.** When your self-talk informs you that other people or things cause your pain, whether it is anger, frustration, helplessness or fear, your thinking is off base.

"When you take charge of what happens on the inside, you regain your power. If you think you need to stop other people from 'making you mad,' you're going to have to change everyone who could potentially trigger your anger—an endless task!"

"Tell me about it!" Richard smirked. "To date, my efforts to change others have been futile, but I don't like being the one who has to do the changing, the one who has to do all the work! What about them? I want them to do their fair share," Richard complained. He seemed tense and squirmed in his seat. It looked as though he was having difficulty finding a comfortable position.

"The parts of your life which don't work for you now can be changed by simply doing the work we are discussing. That no one else has to change in order for you to feel good is probably the best news you will ever hear. *You* are the one who will have to *do the work* for *you* to be empowered.

"It is unnecessary to run away from life and keep cycling into the hopelessness you are experiencing now. **There is something you can do and doing it is *your* healing process!** As far as others are concerned, if they are in pain they will have to find their own willingness. *They* will have to do their own changing and engage in the process themselves in order to experience *their healing and empowerment*—in order to change *their* lives."

Two simple rules to remember are:

☑ **If I'm in pain, I'm in error.**

☑ **Anyone who is in pain has work to do.**

Richard's confusion about how to create new experiences in life without changing other people is typical of the way most of us see the world. In every difficulty between people, there are two conflicting realities, two people in pain, two who must take responsibility for themselves in order to heal. A common avoidance tactic is pointing the finger to what someone else has not done while leaving one's own work incomplete.

> ⚷ KEY THOUGHT—Let's put away our magnifying glasses and get out our mirrors. It is time to stop criticizing others and focus on ourselves.

Richard let me know that what I said seemed to make sense, but he was confused by the fact that his negative feelings only happened when he was with the women in his life. His hostility seemed to quiet as he expressed skepticism. I talked about how feelings are easier to hide when there is no one around to trigger them. I reminded him of the bridge analogy and that the bridge remains down when there is nothing to trigger its potential to elevate. I informed him of the work of a former IBM research scientist, Marcel Vogel, who was able to measure the high energy waves that leave the mind when we think a thought. "Richard, I like to call those energy waves the 'psychic megaphone.' **Every reality in your mind sets up an energy wave to attract people who are in tune with that reality. The people we attract then trigger the reality within us, but the trigger does not *cause* our feelings, it only resonates what is already there."**

Richard and I explored just whom he was calling with his psychic megaphone to serve as his trigger. The primary area of examination was his long history of unhappy involvements with women. As we did so, he hooked into some strong emotions while he talked about his list of unresolved resentments.

"I have drawn in some real winners! The women I am attracted to seem very warm and loving—for a while. Then all of a sudden they become distant and, no matter what I do, I can't seem to get their attention. That makes me frustrated and sad, then I get really angry and attack!" He was visibly agitated as he spoke.

Richard had blamed the women in his life for his feelings of sadness and anger and was confused about why he only felt those feelings when he was in relationships. "How," he wondered out loud, "could it not be their fault?"

"Once you grasp the ability the mind has to set up and distort its images, I think you will see how perception can be so far off base. One of the difficulties in understanding and seeing through our distortions is that we attempt to gain clarity without cleaning up the device that is doing the distorting—the mind!

"One historical method used to get past the inherent distortions in the mind is the parable, a word which in Aramaic means 'parallel meaning.' A parable engages the mind with its literal meaning while the underlying message, which cannot be directly taught, bypasses the intellect and is understood by the part of us that is more than a mind. I'd like to share a parable designed to assist in grasping how limiting current human beliefs are. It also helps build the brain cells necessary for functioning in a totally different way—with different realities guiding us."

dr. michael ryce

3

WORDS COULD NEVER SAY...

"Imagine a two-dimensional creature, one that knows only length and width. There is no height in her world. Length and width are the only dimensions she sees.

"We want to play basketball with this creature. As we introduce the basketball into her space, imagine yourself in her position. You have a limited view of what is going on in the world; you can see only the length and width of things. Your ability to perceive is narrowed by one dimension from your normal human perception. From a flat context, a three-dimensional perspective and understanding is *impossible*.

"Richard, when the basketball is moved into the two-dimensional creature's space, what does she see?"

"She is going to experience a flat line. Actually, perhaps just a dot at first, then a series of flat planes until she gets to the other end of the ball when it becomes a dot again."

"Notice, Richard, that our two-dimensional friend, while she experiences something, experiences something that does not exist. When she sees a series of flat planes pass by, she sees something take place that never actually happened. A basketball is not a series of *flat planes*, though she experiences it as such, it is a *spherical object*.

"Now, let's go one step further. The two-dimensional creature has invented, in her experience of the basketball, a thing called time. For you and me, the basketball is just there; there is no experience of time involved. Since her perception can not encompass the whole ball at once, she experiences one part of the ball first and another last. This is how time is invented. Suddenly, a thing that for you and me is a single experience requiring no time becomes time-bound. What for us happens in the same instant seems to be a number of different, separate experiences for a creature with limited perception.

"You might imagine that the two-dimensional creature names her separate experiences. She calls the first Joe, another Mary. Each aspect of the ball, as it comes into her awareness, becomes something different. Its size, shape, nature and character change with each perspective. As a result of *limited perception* she invents a world that doesn't exist!

"That can be a tough one for the human mind to grasp and is an important principle to recognize; *if* your perception is limited, you can experience something that never happened *except as a perceptual reality in your mind*. **We are often taught to experience perceptual realities that don't exist anywhere but in our minds.** We are also taught to believe that those realities are true in the world outside of us when they are not!

"Imagine our two-dimensional friend's parents teaching her about basketballs. She has read the history books. She has studied the 'basketball experiences' of all two-dimensional creatures. What does all this past speak of, but events that never happened? A written chronicle of an experience that doesn't exist does not make it true. Basketballs simply do not exist as a series of events separated by time, they only *appear* to exist that way because of *limited perception*. Whenever one dimension is missing in a perceptual system, the output of the system is always distorted.

"Is it possible, Richard, that having limited perception about an event, *we* could experience things that didn't happen?"

"I guess so," he replied.

"How do I go about assisting our two-dimensional friend to bypass the false realties in her mind so she can experience an actual basketball? Do you think that if you and I talk with her and explain what a basketball is really about, we will be able to get her to come and play basketball with us? Is our explanation going to make any sense?

"When we tell her that her experience never happened, do you think she might be offended?" I asked.

Richard grinned, "I can hear her now. 'Who do you think you are? I have *experienced* the flat planes; I know!'"

"The difficulty, of course, is she *has experienced* the basketball as a series of flat planes," I said. "How do you explain to her that she has seen something that doesn't exist? What do we do with that? Can we teach her about basketballs? Is it possible to give her enough descriptions of a basketball that she will give up all of her two-dimensional history? Her experience? Everything her parents and history have taught her?

"Do you think she will say, 'Okay, I believe you, I've been all wrong.' Not highly likely. Do you think any number of words that she can understand will explain the real meaning of the basketball to her? Obviously not, because her whole vocabulary is based on the limited experience, the distortions, of two-dimensional creatures. Her words only reflect the realities with which she is familiar. There are no words in her language for the three-dimensional perspective of a basketball.

"Think about this in our human terms. Do we have words for what we haven't experienced? No, we only have words for the experiences we have *in common*. If we were Floridians who had never seen snow, how many different descriptive words might we have for it? Perhaps three or four, which would be adequate for our experiences with snow. We wouldn't have a lot of descriptors because snow is not a major part of our lives.

"If we go to Alaska and interview an Eskimo, things would be different. I understand they have some seventy-plus words for snow—an important part of their environment. If, in Alaska, I'm going to do some cross country travel and you describe the snow conditions inaccurately, I might use the wrong snowshoes and perish.

"The realities present in a mind and the words used to represent those realities tend to be limited by the experiences of that mind.

"Let's imagine our two-dimensional friend makes the shift and experiences playing basketball. Is there any way she could explain to her friends what a basketball really is? Can you imagine her excitement? She has broken the chain of history and she now comprehends the true meaning of a basketball. She approaches her friends and says, with a display of enthusiasm, 'I finally know the Truth about basketballs, they are... ah... ah... t-they... Wait a minute! There aren't any words in our vocabulary that accurately describe a basketball. How can I speak to you about what I've experienced?' You might imagine her saying things like, 'You know, there are so many things that I want to say to you, but you cannot hear them.'"

Richard broke in, "All the words from our world aren't going to be of any use in her world because the words she knows, though *based* on the same *actuality*, describe a totally *different reality*."

"I agree, and this addresses both your question, 'How can life be so different from the way I perceive it?' and our friend's question, 'How can the basketball be other than a series of flat planes, separated by time?'"

"How do you get around this predicament?" he asked.

"The best way I know is to persuade the two-dimensional creature to *question everything* she has been *taught and experienced* about basketballs. If she can recognize that nothing she has experienced ever happened the way she experienced it, she has a chance of opening to a new perspective. If you can get her to

remove *every reality ever accepted by her mind and oper
view of basketballs, she might make the leap."*

We spoke of the idea, expressed by Einstein, that we live in a four-dimensional world. "Are we, as human beings, *actually* in the position of the two-dimensional creature? Is our basketball called the world? **Are we missing one perceptual dimension?** Does that keep us from experiencing the world as it actually is? If so, could we study enough or would we even have any words about the *actual* world? Are we required to give up all of our experiences from the past in order to step into the Truth about life?"

"What you present is sensible, but I don't comprehend the questions, nor do I have any answers to them. Just trying to think about what you are saying is bewildering," Richard replied.

"I ask these questions not to elicit answers, but to invite you to suspect everything you think you know or have experienced. **Until we accept responsibility and grasp the Truth about life, we make up all sorts of realities that are not true.**

"Many people live in a perceptual world that contains reference points to the actual world, but at the same time is void of the Truth about actuality. Perception is a made-up story which is overlaid on the actual world. This action destroys the ability to experience actuality. People tend to cling tightly to their false perceptions as though life itself depends on them, which in a sense, it does. The false life lived by most people is dependent on keeping the Truth hidden. Hence, Truth is its greatest enemy. This sets up an insane cycle—Truth is required to experience Love and happiness—if Truth is not allowed, Love and happiness are *impossible.* When we deny Truth we engage this insanity cycle and we inflict pain on ourselves and miss out on the gifts life is offering us."

> ☞ KEY THOUGHT—Now that the Truth has been told, there is room for *real Love.*
> Bill C. Davis, the play *Mass Appeal*

> *ALL OUR ACTIVITIES SHOULD BE CENTERED IN TRUTH. TRUTH SHOULD BE THE VERY BREATH OF OUR LIFE. WHEN ONCE THIS STAGE... IS REACHED, ALL OTHER RULES OF CORRECT LIVING WILL COME WITHOUT EFFORT, AND OBEDIENCE TO THEM WILL BE INSTINCTIVE. BUT WITHOUT TRUTH IT IS IMPOSSIBLE TO OBSERVE ANY PRINCIPLES OR RULES OF LIFE.*

Mahatma Gandhi, *India of My Dreams*

4

FEELINGS,
OUR GUIDANCE SYSTEM

Feelings are the primary feedback mechanism for the human being. The goal of this work is to present tools with which to explore life, feelings, and the Truth about the world. Our next goal is to demonstrate how to use these tools and inspire each person we contact to put them to work. Let's look at feelings from a different perspective than the norm.

Feelings come from within. *No one* can make you feel angry, sad, afraid or anything else; others, however, can certainly trigger the *cause* of the feelings you hold. It takes a significant shift of mind to see that the cause of pain is internal. Grasping the Truth of this premise is difficult for most people because they have spent their entire lives investing in the belief that someone else has the power to make them feel.

The first step required in order to integrate any new idea is to let go of old, conflicting beliefs. **No one can simultaneously take responsibility for his or her life while blaming someone else.** Once the commitment is made to be *response-able*, the output of the internal mechanism is free to change—reality changes.

"Richard, freeing yourself from the belief that any person, place, thing, event or circumstance causes you to feel requires a new look at reality and an undoing of the clouds of the past. When you are angry, you have caused your own anger; when there is fear, the fear is of your own making."

"That's ridiculous! Why would I make myself angry? How could I make myself angry? My feelings are a result of what happens in my life," Richard protested.

"Would you be willing to do an experiment that is designed to give you a direct experience of what causes your feelings?"

"Sure."

"Once you do this exercise, there is no turning back to blame, because its conclusion is so simple. It can be denied, but only temporarily. The direct experience lies in the mind as a seed that will, sooner or later, bear the fruit of responsibility for every aspect of your life."

"I'm really not sure I'm ready for that, but I guess it's time. Let's go for it!"

"Okay. If you would, close your eyes. I'm going to ask you to let yourself feel some feelings. First, let yourself feel sadness. Intensify the sadness. Take a deep breath and let go of your sadness. Let yourself feel anger. Intensify the anger. Take a deep breath and let go of your anger. Go to the feeling of fear. Intensify the fear. Take a deep breath and let go of the fear. Let yourself feel pain. Place your hand wherever you are feeling the pain." Richard placed his hand on his forehead as he held his breath.

"Now, open your eyes.

"Notice where your hand is, Richard. Your hand is showing you where you hold the energy that causes your pain. If you learn how to change that energy, healing happens. If you don't, that is where your disease processes will tend to manifest."

"But... " Richard interjected.

"Let me just go through the rest of the exercise before we get into a discussion. Would you close your eyes again for a moment?

Take a deep breath and let go of the sadness, the fear, the anger and the pain. Let yourself go to the feeling of joy and aliveness, and open your eyes."

"That feels better," he said immediately.

"How did you feel each of the feelings you just had?"

"I recalled an experience that caused those feelings in me previously," he replied.

"What did you do to recall that experience? What specifically was the mechanical process?"

"I'm not sure I understand what you're asking."

"What happened in your mind to get to each of the feelings you just felt?"

"I thought about something that caused those feelings. Is that what you mean?"

"Yes. Notice, to feel a feeling you had to think. You had a thought, right? **Feelings are shadows of thoughts,**" I offered. "In the last two minutes, you had several different feelings, right?"

"Yes."

"Whose thoughts caused those feelings?"

"Mine, I guess," Richard said, looking a little confused, "but I had the feelings because of the event I thought about, not because of the thoughts I had."

"It sure looks that way, but I think it actually works differently, Richard. What was one of the scenes you thought of to feel anger?"

"I just had to think of my wife leaving me and being alone as a result of her action," he said.

"What if you were to think about her leaving and at the same time hold the thought, 'I'm ready to do my whole life differently, what an opportunity to heal!'?"

"I would never think that, michael!"

"After this experience, you might change your mind. Give it a try, see what happens. Get into thinking about her leaving and allow yourself to generate thoughts of excitement about doing your life differently and the opportunity to heal. Think those thoughts as true, exciting thoughts about your life and see what happens."

"I'm not feeling angry. Actually, I feel anticipation about how life can be. Hmm... but it's not true, I am angry with her."

"Notice, Richard, it is your thought about the event, not the event itself that causes your feelings. You can choose to hold onto your angry thoughts, but when you do, *you* get the original, your wife just gets a carbon copy. Your thoughts impact you first. Take notice, she is not here to know what you are thinking, but each thought has an impact on you. **Your feelings inform you of the nature of the impact of the energy of your thoughts on your physiology.** If you are in pain, you are the one who is in error."

"My thoughts cause me to feel... what a novel concept," Richard half mumbled to himself.

"Let's take the principle a step further. If yesterday, last week, last month or last year, you had negative feelings or pain, whose thoughts caused you to feel that pain?"

"Mine," he acknowledged.

"If tomorrow, next week, next month or next year you experience that quality of pain, whose thought will be the cause of your pain?"

"Obviously mine," was his short reply.

"Do you expect to experience pain at some time in the future?" I inquired.

"Of course, won't everyone?"

"I'm not sure it is necessary, Richard. Why would you inflict pain on yourself?"

22   dr. michael ryce

"I-I don't know. Habit, I guess."

"There is only one reason. Insanity."

"You mean I'm insane!?"

"To the degree that we each inflict pain on ourselves, Richard, we are all insane. The world teaches us insane thought systems and, in so doing, it teaches us to destroy ourselves. If we buy in and think insane thinking is normal, we will reach the conclusion that we have no other choice.

"Thoughts, I would offer, are a form of energy. Whenever you put a quality of mind energy into your physiology, you get a feeling that corresponds to that quality. Feelings are your feedback mechanism and tell you whether you are engaging in constructive or destructive mind energy.

"When you make a mistake, the feeling is negative. I would offer that you and I are made in the image of Love, and there is no other reality that belongs in the human experience. Any other reality is a violation of the human structure, and we destroy ourselves when we focus on dis-integrative energies.

☞ KEY THOUGHT—If I'm in pain, I'm in error.

"We build our realities, literally, with each piece of mind energy in which we engage. **The mind has the amazing capacity to turn our mind energy into the *actual* images we see.** If you put hate, fear, anger, anguish, terror, criticism, condemnation, gossip, slander or vengeance into your structure, that mind energy will turn into an image in your brain. If you're in denial, you'll think the image is about somebody else, though *it comes from your physiology.* Every image your mind produces explains where *you* are. If you can't own that, you'll never be able to see yourself accurately and correction will be impossible. One of the goals of this work is to provide a variety of tools for correction."

"Just what do you mean by tools, michael?"

"Tools are concrete techniques or actions you can use to resolve upsets or patterns at the moment they occur. They are designed to provide a way to assist in creating joy and unloading the burdens most people accumulate in the course of their daily lives. For instance, taking responsibility is a tool. When you project responsibility onto another, the mind shows you they are your problem. When you use the tool of responsibility, you resolve that projection because your mind will shift what it shows you about both them and yourself. Being aware that feelings are a guidance system is another tool. When you use that awareness you tend to look at yourself accurately and are more likely to see your self truly rather than blame others when your upset surfaces.

"A few of the many other tools presented in this work include 'My Commitment,' Breathing, Awareness, and Forgiveness. I could go on with a long list but each tool will unfold in its own time."

"I'm confused," Richard said solemnly.

"I understand. It is a lot to absorb all at once, but the principles of this work are really quite simple. **The seeming complexity and confusion of learning this new way of thinking come from the habit of holding onto old beliefs, which makes it difficult to integrate new ideas.** The confusion does not come from the principles themselves.

> ☞ KEY THOUGHT—Truth is complex to a complex mind and simple to a simplified mind.

"Did you learn traditional mathematics when you were in school?" Richard nodded. "Have you encountered the new math since then?"

"Yes, I attempted to learn it and teach it to my daughter. Studying it was like going into a foreign world, and I felt pretty stupid when it took me weeks to catch up with her. She was only twelve at the time!"

"That is my point. With this material, you are being introduced to a whole new way of thinking and living, a new world so to speak. You may even get the chance to feel and heal some of that old 'stupid' feeling as you integrate this teaching. There is a saying that, **'You can't do new math with an old math mind.'** In the same way, you cannot simultaneously take responsibility for your life while you blame someone else.

> ☞ KEY THOUGHT—When we respond, we make a conscious choice. When we re-act, we are unconsciously driven by our past. *Respons-ability* is the *ability* to *respond* rather than re-act.

"Once you recognize your feelings are generated by your internal mechanism, you have the key to power over those feelings, and you can take responsibility for them. It is then possible to respond rather than just react to life's triggers. When you are willing and committed to being response-able, you can change the output of your mind and that action will change your reality. The way you feel will no longer be dependent upon any person, place, thing, event or circumstance."

"Ha! That sounds great. What's the catch?" he asked.

"Richard, there is no catch," I replied, "but there are ideas you have to change. For example, you will have to be able to see and deal with your hidden pain.

"You see, Richard, someone can only bring up a painful reality if it's already in your mind; *it has to be there first.* You can pretend that all is well and continue to deny and hide from your issues, but the fact that someone can trigger anger in you is a sure sign that something is hidden.

"Removing realities from the mind is the original meaning of the word 'Forgive.' In this work, when a negative reality is triggered, it is an opportunity to learn *True Forgiveness.*

When pain surfaces, if you are honest and in touch with yourself, you will own the upset and seize the opportunity to release that internal reality—to *Forgive!* Pain functions to inform us of our errors.

"False forgiveness is based on the belief that others are responsible for what we feel, and therefore it tends to reinforce that error. To forgive others, in this manner, for what happens in your mind leaves your pain intact and the opportunity to heal is lost. Making use of every opportunity to heal is an important decision you can make and that decision will immeasurably accelerate your process."

Richard didn't seem convinced. "Thanks, but I'll pass," he said sarcastically, "if I have a painful reality hiding somewhere in my mind, I'd just as soon leave it there, thank you."

> ⊙══╤ KEY THOUGHT—The purpose of life, when we refuse to listen to pain, our warning signal, is to kick us in the limitation. The more we resist listening, the harder life kicks us.

5

THE PURPOSE OF PAIN

Unless a person has tools to support healing in their lives, painful realities remain hidden in their minds and bodies. I wanted to explore with Richard how these stored realities express. I marveled that people who have no idea that there are tools with which they can unload their burdens survive as long as they do.

"I hear, loud and clear, that you would rather not deal with your pain, but allow me to add another piece to the puzzle," I offered. "What you hide from yourself is your dis-ease."

"How did you get from stored, painful realities to disease?!" Richard demanded.

"Physicists tell us everything is energy. Think of the *body* being an energy field instead of physical matter. There are two main categories of energy relative to that field. There is disintegrative energy, which tears the human energy system down and integrative energy which builds the system up."

"What does that have to do with disease?" Richard said.

"Pain is a signal of dis-ease. Not disease, but dis-ease. It tells the system that somewhere within there is something physically, mentally or emotionally out of place. It is not an enemy, but a friend in disguise. When we don't want to listen to the feedback the system gives us, it gets our attention by yelling—*pain!*

"The purpose of pain is to make our ears grow. If we refuse to listen by suppressing the warning, it will grow in intensity. Pain will not be ignored! Sooner or later, it gets our full attention and we follow its guidance to correction, or we die. This applies to physical, mental, emotional and relationship pain.

"Getting rid of pain without dealing with its message is like cutting the wires to the bell on a fire alarm. The fire alarm screams out to get your attention, to tell you there is a problem. It demands, 'LISTEN TO ME.' If you refuse to listen by shutting down the feedback, things do quiet down, but the fire still rages somewhere. Sooner or later, the fire will break through and make you aware that it is burning. The longer it takes to recognize where the fire is, the more difficult it will probably be to extinguish. Killing the bell certainly has nothing to do with putting the fire out."

"Pain is just a bell, warning us that we need to look at something?" Richard asked in amazement. "I always thought you were just supposed to take a pill to make pain go away and that was how you got well. That's what I was taught!"

"That thinking will sure sell a lot of pills, but shutting down the alarm without dealing with the fire that's burning will lead to total destruction. Obviously, pain held anywhere in tissue does not contribute to the health of that tissue or any part of the system. The only reason for pain, 100% of the time, is the disintegrative energy that invites us to look deeper into ourselves and deal with whatever we have hidden there.

"Medical research is proving that *every* cell in the *body* stores information. Our dis-ease and our pain come from the energy introduced into tissue by the negative realities we store there and the drugs we use to keep those realities suppressed. The secondary cause of pain is the lifestyle we choose to keep ourselves in a weakened condition."

"What?" Richard blared. "You've got to be ki
would *purposely* weaken themselves?"

"Think about it, Richard. You can't suppress anything in an
energy system that is at full vitality. In order to suppress, something
has to shut down the flow of energy in the system so that whatever
is hidden remains that way.

"Show me someone who takes a drug for, let's say,
depression. If you remove their drug, what happens? They begin to
remember what has been suppressed by the drug and go back into
that depression, right?"

"Well, that means the drug worked, doesn't it? Without it, they
feel depressed. With it, they feel better." Richard rubbed his chin
and appeared to be struggling to understand.

"Depends on what you mean by worked, Richard. If sweeping
something under the rug is your definition of 'worked,' drugs are
doing their job. The action of most drugs, legal or illegal, including
caffeine, nicotine, sugar, alcohol or junk food, is to lower the vitality
of the system sufficiently so that the pain we desire to suppress
remains out of conscious awareness.

"Notice, I said 'out of conscious awareness,' not gone or
cured. It only means we are no longer aware of it. If we use drugs
to suppress pain and the *cause* of the pain is still intact; sooner or
later it will surface somewhere in the system, often under the guise
of a 'side effect.' **What you can't see or feel, you cannot
heal.** However, pain is not required, it is only a motivator. If we
consciously choose to motivate ourselves, then instead of 'no pain,
no gain,' our lives will be 'no pain, no pain.'"

> ☞ KEY THOUGHT—Life is designed to give
> us as many opportunities as we need to heal. If
> we don't take the initiative and do our inner work,
> life often motivates us through pain.

"Does that mean I should never take drugs?" Richard asked.

"There are benefits to the use of drugs in that you have better short-term function when you keep pain suppressed, but true healing is impossible in that state. **Drugs in the hands of a true healer can be used to temporarily control threatening symptoms and they can save a life. However, they don't heal, though they can buy time to do the necessary inner work of healing."**

I went on to reinforce that healing does not come from a drug any more than a fire is put out by cutting the wires on the bell. He seemed to relate to the idea that drugs shut down the highly tuned mechanism of feelings and rob us of our feedback. **"The mind cannot show us what we are unwilling to see and therefore distorts every situation where there is denial.** Drugs simply reinforce the blockages denial creates, they are like a physical form of denial. If one does not have and use tools with which to heal, drugs tend to become a way of life, a one-way ticket to degeneration!"

I shared with Richard a poem that sums up perfectly for me the whole topic of dis-ease and our part in it:

EACH MOMENT

Each moment of Love,
Each moment of giving,
Each moment of joy,
Is a moment of living.

Each moment of anger,
Each moment of lying,
Each moment of fear,
Is a moment of dying.

All our moments add together,
Like the digits in a sum,
And the answer tells us plainly,
Whether life or death will come.

Anonymous

6

WHAT IS REALITY?

Richard expressed relief at understanding more about what drove his mind and caused his pain. He explained it had never occurred to him that what showed up in his mind—his reality—could possibly be different from what happened in the world—actuality. He acknowledged that he lived totally unaware that denial could distort realities in the mind so completely. Grasping that principle struck a chord of recognition for him, and he volunteered an example.

"I had never conceived before that what happens in the world could possibly be different from what shows up in my mind. The other day I was in a restaurant enjoying a steaming cup of coffee when the waitress came by and took it. I didn't give her the chance to explain," he continued sheepishly, "I just snapped at her before I saw the fresh cup in her other hand. She had seen me spill the coffee in the saucer and was attempting to keep me from making a mess of my clean suit.

"I have never thought in these terms before, but what you are saying helps me make sense of that situation. When I turned and saw her picking up my cup, I thought, 'Don't touch my coffee!' I was quick to attack. I now realize her reality was probably something like, 'Uh-oh, that cup is about to drip! I'd better grab it!'" Richard concluded.

With the idea of bringing the train of thought full circle, I offered, "Your underlying reality was probably something like, 'People take things from me!' For her, it was likely, 'I take care of people.' In the meantime, the actuality was that she simply picked up a dripping cup." As we continued to focus on his experience with the waitress and the *reality* in him that was being triggered by this event, his insight deepened.

Who is responsible for the realities
that come from your mind?

WHAT IS REALITY?

"Now I see why people in my life are confused by my behavior. I am quick to accuse and they often have no idea why I'm upset. I understand now that my upset is a reality in my head. I'm grasping the idea that my reaction to the waitress didn't have anything to do with the actuality that happened, except that it was a trigger. I'm sure my reality didn't even remotely resemble the one that was happening for her."

This initial insight provided Richard with a new perspective on actuality, his own and others' internal reality structures and his responsibility for his life. He had understood the concept of a "trigger" and was delighted. "I feel great!"

> ⊙━ KEY THOUGHT—We have been trained to think that giving up responsibility for ourselves is easier than being responsible. It is not.

"Good work, Richard. It's exciting to see through new eyes, isn't it? In my experience, most people think, 'Everyone is experiencing the same thing I am; why don't they understand me?' The Truth is that at every moment every person is experiencing a different reality, and seldom do our realities match exactly. **If you don't make room in your heart and mind for other people's realities to be different, especially in your intimate relationships, there is going to be trouble!"**

"Looking at things from that perspective, it amazes me that we even start to get along!" Richard said in an exasperated tone. Silence filled the space as we mulled over that idea.

Suddenly a smile broke the tension in his face, "I'm really starting to understand! Let me see if I can recap what I'm thinking. I'm still a little confused, but bear with me, I need to clarify this. The waitress, and the thousand other people I've done this to, did something that in their reality was positive—something Loving. The actual event between us was neutral; after all, picking up a cup of coffee is just picking up a cup of coffee. She was trying to help, but her action was a trigger for my reality, 'They are taking something away from me.' I attacked her to protect myself from losing something—a reality that was happening only in my own head!"

Richard became quiet; all animation disappeared. Tears rolled down his reddened face and he could hardly speak.

"What's happening, Richard?" I asked quietly.

"I-I'm realizing this happened all the time between my mother and me. I'd do something I thought she would appreciate and instead I got yelled at or beat up for it. I never understood why! No matter how hard I tried, I could never get it right. Living with her was like walking through a minefield."

Several still moments passed before he spoke again.

"I wonder how many people I have destroyed with the same behavior? How many times have I treated others like that and not realized what I was doing? Man, I don't think there are enough apologies in the world for the people I've acted that out with. Do I feel stupid," he mumbled to himself.

Another long silence followed. I finally spoke. "Sounds like perhaps you felt destroyed by your mother."

"N-no, no! I Love my mother, why would you say that?"

"As I listened to your clarification process, which was very powerful, you keyed into at least one of the reasons you attack so readily. You do it to protect what is yours. Your next step was to see that attacking was a pattern you learned from your mother. Listening to your perceptions of the interaction with her tells me a lot about the content of your mind."

When I explained to Richard that **the perceptual output of a mind always tells more about the content of the perceiving mind than about the perceived world,** it made sense to him. He acknowledged that he had felt devastated by his mother and, in spite of pretending that they have a great relationship, he avoids her, even to this day.

As I talked him through his fear of feeling sadness about what he had uncovered, helping to create a safe place for him to be honest with himself, he spoke again of his fear of being destroyed by what might surface.

Richard's fear of being destroyed was an old reality that needed to be exposed fully in order to be healed. I assured him that it was safe to look at whatever came to his mind. I invited him to be aware that a memory of pain is just a memory and he did not need to re-empower his old pain as though it were true, present-moment pain. He had survived the trauma when he first felt it and locked the experience into his *body*; he would survive its release as the old energy moved out of his system. Within moments, through simple breathing and accepting that he was safe, Richard was feeling better and seemed surprised at how much easier it had become to breathe. "What happened?" he asked, amazed at the relief he was suddenly feeling.

"Breathing through the surfacing of old, hidden feelings allows their release. I suspect people will find you easier to get along with in the future, and you will probably see an easing in your relationship with your mother."

"What a relief!" he sighed. "It's interesting to observe how these issues relate to each other. This really takes concentration and work, doesn't it?"

"Yes, and **it takes courage to face yourself and be vulnerable enough to feel your true feelings and honest enough to look at your real thoughts.**

> ⚷ KEY THOUGHT—Life is an opportunity to heal. Use it well.

"I think the most important piece of work you've done in the last few minutes was the next link you made; the thought you 'destroyed' people by attacking them needlessly. Did you notice that insight came on the heels of 'Living with my mom was like walking through a minefield'?

"That sequence of thoughts said to me that, as a child, there was a good chance you felt destroyed by what you perceived as your mother's attacks. It was probably too much for a young mind to confront, so the belief remained hidden until this moment. In the denial of that reality your mind showed you only evidence of a Loving mother and, at the same time, blamed her for your hurt feelings."

Richard's inability to look directly at his thoughts of blame caused them to surface when he least expected. They would run out of control and cause his actions to be out of proportion with the situations he faced. His blame thoughts became generalized. His reaction, attacking the waitress, for example, was generalized from the realities he learned from his early interactions with a mother who attacked to protect herself. This dynamic was the source of the emotional explosions that drove people away, the type of reverberations that often go on for decades after the original reason for blaming has passed.

"The belief that someone else can be responsible for the output of your mind is called projection. If my suspicion is true you attempted to keep the thought that you were destroyed by your mother hidden by projecting it onto yourself. My clue, as I listened, was when you said, 'I destroyed others.'"

"I'm not sure I'm connecting it all together as you are, but it is a relief to be on this side of those feelings. It seems that it will be easier to be gentle with others."

What Richard had just gone through is called *process*. Holding the space of safety and Love allows an unraveling of the jumbled unconscious realities that one holds in his or her mind. Rarely does one realize the dynamics that run beneath the surface when a decision is made or one compulsively engages in behavior they would rather avoid. The mind becomes free of its conflicts when we allow process to happen.

"In the past, if thoughts and feelings like this surfaced for you, it was probably in the context of conflict and anger, which just reinforced your pain and upset. That continuous reinforcement makes it more difficult to confront feelings directly. **It is having a Loving space while issues are surfacing that shifts the energy into a healing mode.**

"Are you willing to continue?" Richard nodded. "You grew up behaving toward others as you perceived your mother did toward you, probably because you saw mom as 'successful' enough to model your behavior after her. That behavior worked to control you, but did it endear your mother to you?"

"No! I hated it when she did that. It drove me away from her."

"So it accomplished the goal of controlling you but you detested being controlled. You hated your mother's behavior, but have you become just like her? Earlier you said another wife was leaving. Has anyone ever told you they felt driven away by you?" I inquired.

"How did you know that?" he asked.

"The same way I figured out you felt destroyed by your mother, but let's hold that issue for a moment. I suggest you notice that controlling behavior does not serve you. It tends to destroy your relationships."

> ○━┳ KEY THOUGHT—We tend to become that which we hate.

Richard paused. "Hmm, this certainly gives me a lot to think about. I'm really going to have to spend some time sorting through this, but I want to understand how you figured all this out from the little I have said."

"Okay, let's look at feeling destroyed by your mother. It appears that it was easier to admit that you destroyed people than to think of her doing that to you. If you believed treating others the way your mother treated you destroyed them, it makes sense that, in your mind, she did the same when she behaved that way toward you. Let's keep in mind that 'destroyed' is a perceptual reality, probably a very complex one which, at this moment, we will not try to break down.

"It's more important, at this stage, that you be responsible for accepting that pattern and modeling your behavior after hers rather than trying to blame your behavior on her. I see many people who take inventory of everyone else's faults, but never acknowledge their role in adopting those faults as their own. This leads to more blame and is a justification many use to avoid accountability. It is a great excuse for staying in old patterns, letting oneself off the hook and not having to change.

"With your waitress story you clarified the difference between actuality, reality and how the mind produces evidence to back up its preconceived notions and create its experiences. You and the waitress experienced the same *actuality* or *external* event. However, your mind selected different evidence and built a reality from it. From that event her mind selected information and assembled it to present a radically different view of the situation. *Your mind* presented a reason to *destroy* while *hers* saw an *opportunity* for service. Notice how each of your individual mind-sets led to divergent experiences."

> ☒━┳ KEY THOUGHT—What do you believe about yourself to create what is happening in your life today?

Richard had unraveled the string of unconscious realities that drove his behavior and led to his need to attack and protect himself. He had reached into the core of this work and healed major issues. **We define healing as the surfacing and letting go of the dis-integrative energies of unconsciousness and trauma.** Who would think spilling coffee in a restaurant could lead to dealing with what is perhaps one of the deepest issues of someone's life? **Every conflicting situation offers the same precious opportunity if you are willing to see it in the context of healing and allow your mind to construct a healing reality!**

dr. michael ryce

7

THE EVIDENTIAL MIND

We went on in our discussion, exploring the "Evidential Mind." Richard experienced his relationships with almost everyone as unpredictable and threatening to his power. He asked, "Why is it others make us feel what we don't want to feel?"

"The mind can only give you information supported by your internal reality structure. If your core belief is 'I am powerless and get attacked by women,' your mind must process your experiences with women in a way that matches that reality. Any information not in sync with that belief is blocked," I answered.

We discussed the idea that the mind is an evidential device and can access only the information one is willing to see. It then uses that information for building its realities which are the mind's *picture* of actuality. When required information is blocked, it is impossible to build an accurate reality. **If Truth is not allowed, the mind cannot reflect the Truth.**

"Richard, when you deny involvement in what happens, in effect, you instruct your mind to hide information relating to your responsibility in that event. The mind does not show you realities contrary to what it believes, because data inconsistent with its deeply held opinions is blocked or gated out.

"The mind has no choice when denied access to information or providing uncalled for data. It sees things that didn't happen if a belief that is different from actuality is triggered. When a belief is resonated by an event in the world, the brain cells that hold that *belief* will fill in data that is not present in the *actuality*. The data filled in will show up in the *mind's reality* as if it were part of the actual *external* event. Our belief systems, until purged of unconsciousness, tend to hold us in an hypnotic-like state.

○━┳ KEY THOUGHT—"It is the theory that decides what can be observed." Albert Einstein

---

"The mind can only follow your instructions to hide what you do not want to see and see what your B.S.—Belief System—calls for. **Gaining access to denied and therefore hidden information and undoing false beliefs are the keys to healing what is at the root of most repeated experiences.** Here are a couple of examples that illustrate the point.

"In a laboratory experiment, cats were implanted with electrodes in the area of the brain that responded to sound. A device that created a clicking noise was placed close to the cat's ear. Each time the experimenters would click the device, the cat's brain registered the sound.

"A mouse in a bell jar was placed in front of the cat. With the cat's attention and senses set on the mouse, sensitive electronic equipment showed the clicking sound no longer registered in the cat's brain. All evidence of the clicking was blocked, or gated out of the cat's awareness. It appears that only evidence that was important to the cat at the moment gained admittance to its awareness."

"How does that translate in human terms?" he inquired.

"The implications are many, especially in relationships. A computer analogy allows us to look deeper into the Evidential Mind's impact on human function. Consider a computer. It is incapable of choice and can only display information as directed.

40

The person operating the computer selects or creates the programs that run on it. Since the computer can only follow directions and display information it has access to, the information available to the operator is limited by the program that is operating.

"Like a computer, the mind can use only programmed, available information in building a *reality* about the *actuality* on which it is focused. When a 'program' is run in a mind, the information the mind can access and the quality of reality available are predetermined by the directions from that program. This fact is commonly recognized and called a bias, slant, mind-set or prejudice.

"If a mind's 'blame program' reads, *'Find the guilty party and make sure it is someone else,'* the reality showing up in that mind can only reflect evidence that is contained in brain cells and is consistent with the program. All other information, internal or external, is gated or blocked out of awareness. It is simply not available for use in building the mind's current reality. If no consistent information is resonated by the actuality being focused upon, the mind will hallucinate the needed evidence out of its past and attach it to the reality generated. *Ever have someone 'see' you do something you didn't do or 'hear' you say something you did not say?*

"A computer must be reprogrammed, or a new program must be loaded in order to access information that is different from what is currently available. In a similar fashion, we must direct our minds to close the 'blame program' and open the 'responsibility program' if we are to see situations, others or ourselves differently.

"If your mind-set or 'program' is 'I'm right, you're wrong! It's settled! Why argue?' Your mind can only use information proving you're right in building its reality about you. It can only use information that proves another's error to build a reality about them. **Any bias renders the mind incapable of providing accurate information about the actual world.**"

> ☞ KEY THOUGHT—My mind can only show me *my reality*. It may or may not match *actuality,* but it always matches what is going on *inside* of me.

I explained to Richard that my conclusion from these ideas and from my observation of human behavior is that **the mind only permits into awareness information that supports its goals and prejudices. All other information is hidden.** If we hold an emotionally charged goal of being right, the mind withholds all evidence that would show the Truth of a situation—that we have made a mistake. The errors we refuse to acknowledge in ourselves, we blame on others.

Blaming someone else for what goes on in our minds and using our internally hidden information to build our mind's image of "them" is called projection. Projection of our internal process is the main block to healing. When we project, we take what is internal and attempt to place it outside ourselves, thus cutting ourselves off from *Forgiving* what is hidden.

"I know I project because I do experience identical realities repeatedly. I'm grasping that those scenarios are coming from my own mind, but I don't understand how that interrupts healing. How does projection work in relationships?" Richard queried.

8

WHAT IS PROJECTION?

To answer his question about projection, more information on how the mind sets up what it sees was necessary. Once its reality is structured, the mind tends to see only in terms of its own contents and pre-programmed filters. It tends to place the meanings it contains on anything similar to its past. **To a hammer the whole world looks like a nail.**

"What is this, Richard?"

"A house, of course."

"The Truth is, it is just lines on paper. A man from the jungle who had lived in nothing but caves, would not look at those lines and say, 'Oh, that house has smoke coming out of the chimney.' He does not have that meaning, that reality stored in his mind. He has no brain cells that contain that information. For him there is no house in the lines on the page. 'House' is a reality contained in and projected outward from the mind of the observer and only an observer with a house in their past would call the lines on the page a house."

"You mean there is nothing out there? It's all in my mind?" Richard seemed baffled.

"No, the lines on the page are there, the *external world exists*. The point I'm making is that until we become aware, the objective world is just a framework upon which we project or hang what we have filed away in our minds.

"Imagine a child whose home life was miserable, a life of severe abuse. If he sees these lines on the page, what might happen? His blood pressure might rise, his eyes will probably bulge slightly, and he might be preparing to run. *He has given the lines a meaning from his past—a meaning contained in his mind.*

"Another child who loved lying on the couch in front of the fireplace while mom or dad rubbed her back sees the lines on our page. Images of wonderful food and family events might be triggered as she projects the *meaning her mind contains upon the identical framework.* Her mind does not generate a reason to run."

Richard was beginning to grasp the subtle concept that **a reality seen through a mind is internal to the perceiving mind.** He fed back to me his understanding that as you look at the lines on the paper, your mind instantly gives a meaning to them; the lines themselves have no meaning other than what your mind projects. I completed this aspect of the discussion with the idea, once again, that **projection results from the belief that *someone else* is responsible for the output of your mind.** When that belief is held, the mind uses whatever internal information is triggered by another for building a reality about that person. Our denied and suppressed attribute shows up as part of the image our mind builds of them. The mind successfully documents that our pain belongs to them—they are the cause of what we feel.

"The mind is actually a prism through which we view life. If there is any distortion—any kind of resentment or negative feeling—that resentment or negative feeling clouds perception and colors our view of the world. This is why the *First Law* of Seeing is

Love. A mind that constantly holds the condition of Love, regardless of circumstance, distorts nothing and is incapable of projection.

"When there is a distortion within the mind, we live within its meaning. If anyone who remotely resembles a person we hold a grievance against comes into awareness through our senses, we will instantly project our reality onto them. We tend to believe that it is they who are the source of our grievance and pain, rather than accepting responsibility for the content of our own minds. This blocks the ability to heal what someone triggers in us and leads to experiencing the same realities repeatedly. Only when we take responsibility can we change the foundations of our perception.

"Denial keeps the source of our pain hidden. We, as human beings, are usually taught to interact in relationships in a way that guarantees a cycle of repeated experiences. The first step in keeping that cycle going is to deny any involvement in causing our own pain. Then blame another and instruct that person in how he or she should change. If they refuse, we are taught to punish them to force change. If punishment doesn't work, we often leave or throw them out of our lives. This formula is guaranteed. If you use it, you can rest assured that someone who knows exactly how to access and show you the hidden parts of your mind will soon be knocking on your door . . . AGAIN!

"It is interesting to note that we project in order to avoid pain and by doing so lock inside ourselves the very thing we are attempting to avoid. This is a good definition of insanity."

> ☞ KEY THOUGHT—Projection results from the belief that someone else is responsible for *my* thoughts, *my* feelings, *my* reality—and the output of *my* mind.

Richard slowly fed back to me, "If I understand correctly, by blaming you, I expect you to be responsible for my reality even though it all comes from inside my own mind. If I try to control you through punishment, I'm kidding myself into believing that by changing you I will never be forced to experience my pain again. Is that what you are saying?"

"Yes. **Changing someone else will not—cannot change your reality. Only you can initiate and carry out that process, only you can change what is in your mind.** It also takes a lot of energy to keep the *lie* of projection in place and prevent the Truth from entering your awareness."

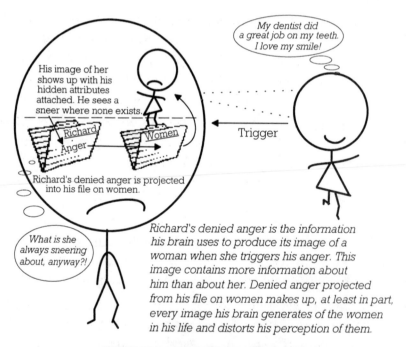

Richard's denied anger is the information his brain uses to produce its image of a woman when she triggers his anger. This image contains more information about him than about her. Denied anger projected from his file on women makes up, at least in part, every image his brain generates of the women in his life and distorts his perception of them.

THE PROJECTION GAME

"Put that way, michael, I can see the conflict is in my own thinking. I am trying to achieve an unreachable goal and I get so frustrated I exhaust myself. That is so obvious now and I see what has been zapping my energy!" he reflected. "A friend who is a medical doctor recently told me the most common complaint he hears is about lack of energy. He called it chronic fatigue. I'm starting to understand the source of my tiredness. It's like I've been carrying a one ton weight on my shoulders!"

Richard's tendency to run from conflict provided an example for us to examine the dynamics of projection in his life. I explained: "In a relationship based on projection, each believes the other is responsible for his or her projections and carries their hidden, unhealed upsets as a burden. As a result, each mind has a distorted picture of what is actually happening. This distortion results from Blockage of Truth. The mind projects its own errors onto others and cannot see the Truth about itself.

"The mind has unconsciously used its hidden information to build its image of 'them'. We then pretend that our mind's image is a true and accurate picture of the outside world, when it is only a true and accurate picture of what is happening inside of us. It is just a projection of a condition in our own minds.

"When projection occurs, each person expects others to be responsible for his or her thoughts and realities. Each, in effect, wants the other to change his or her mind. As a result, *each* mind distorts its picture of actuality. The distortion results from Blockage of Truth, which is inherent in the act of projecting. The blocked mind experiences powerlessness because it is cut off from Truth, not because another person has the power. We have done ourselves a major disservice when we project, for we have cut ourselves off from the part of our belief system that needs healing."

Richard almost exploded with excitement as he expressed his thoughts. **"You mean it's all an inside job?!"** he tendered. "As long as I project—pretend that you are responsible for my reality—I block the Truth? Being out of touch with the Truth is at the root of my feelings of powerlessness? Once I grasp that it is my holding on that keeps me re-experiencing the same painful scenarios, I can get out of the cycle by using the tools?

"This is actually starting to make sense! I'm surprised, I feel hopeful—like there is something I can do!" he continued, his voice sounding a little lighter. "I've always been terrified around women and never did understand how I could feel that helpless in front of someone who was eight inches shorter and 60 pounds lighter than I am.

"Now, I see that whenever I hold a reality based on the belief that I am powerless, anyone who triggers that reality in me can make me believe I am powerless—is that right?"

Richard was pretty close in his understanding. **No one can actually make another feel anything. However, others can trigger the internal mechanism, and whatever is there will surface.** "Richard, if you have a reality called 'powerlessness' and someone stimulates that belief about yourself, you will experience the effects of that belief as feelings of powerlessness. Keep in mind that you feel something because that reality is within you. No one can make you experience a reality that you haven't already created within yourself.

> ⊙━╥ KEY THOUGHT—We tend to dislike and resist in others what we suppress in ourselves.

"If you mistake 'them' as the cause of your reality, of your upset and of your feelings, you will seem to be a 'victim' of them and tend to dislike or hate them. If you know how feelings are formulated within yourself and take corrective action, each painful situation will simply be your opportunity to heal."

"Why should I forgive them?" Richard quipped.

"I didn't suggest forgiving *them*, Richard, I suggested forgiving the realities in your mind. *True Forgiveness* does not mean letting someone else off the hook; you *can't* forgive anyone for anything. *True Forgiveness* **is a tool for changing realities in your own mind,** but I'd like to take up that topic in more detail later."

9

BLOCKAGE OF TRUTH

"Richard, many of the ideas in this work are difficult to accept at first because the brain cells must be built to see them. Have you noticed how much we resist being made aware of the Truth of things we would rather hide from ourselves?

"Most people can think of many examples in their lives when they have tried to point out what someone was in denial about and did not want to hear. Does it sometimes seem unbelievable how difficult it is for a person to see what to others is so obvious? This dynamic is called *Blockage Of Truth*.

"**If you pretend your life is the responsibility of others and that you have nothing to do with creating the painful emotions and the repetitious conflicts in your life, you tell yourself a dis-empowering lie and in so doing hide the Truth from yourself.** Many things influence our view of life and relationships, often without our awareness. Family patterns, parental messages, blame, projection, old behavior patterns, Blockage of Truth and false forgiveness all play their part in how we interact with each other. **Relationships don't die, they must be killed.** Let's look at how some of these dynamics play out in a typical conflict. Notice how predictable the results are when people act out of their old patterns, refuse to look at themselves and 'forgive' each other.

dr. michael ryce

"Since most people blame others for what happens to them, they 'forgive' by letting the other person off the hook."

"What if I need to be forgiven for something I've done?"

"We have been taught an error about forgiveness, Richard. The act you are asking about is called pardoning.

"If you feel you have made an error and wish to be excused for your error, you have need of pardon, not forgiveness. Until we learn the true meaning of forgiveness, we substitute pardoning and think that forgiveness has occurred. The act of pardoning does nothing to change the internal reality structure of the person doing the pardoning. It leaves the painful internal reality in the mind in place, ready to be triggered . . . AGAIN! It also means that the person who is pardoning will usually try to control those he or she pardons so they will not trigger pain again."

"When people 'forgive' each other, using the misunderstood form of forgiveness, they let each other 'off the hook.' Then each mind still has its invisible blockages and painful realities. The only way that what has been blocked in a mind becomes visible is as pain and upset projected into its image of others.

"Each mind, then keeps its distance, viewing the other as a source of pain. Each tends to avoid a real relationship with 'them' because they fear their internalized pain will be triggered . . . AGAIN. **The more often either of them 'forgives' the other in this erroneous sense, the more likely they are to think of 'them' as the problem, and the more separation they will create."**

Richard was agitated at being challenged one more time with the idea that he caused his own pain and proceeded to read me the riot act. "Well, that's the way it is. Other people have always been the cause of almost every problem! If only they would listen and think logically!" he shrieked, as he momentarily forgot how the dynamic of projection works.

"I suppose thinking logically means thinking like you do?" I volleyed. "That reminds me of the old definition of a genius: someone who agrees with me. Thinking someone else is to blame is a good defense, Richard, but remember, you are the only one who has been there *every* time—you are the common link in *every* event."

I went on to refresh Richard's memory, something we all need from time to time. "Whether or not we are aware of it, whether or not we choose responsibility, we are involved in setting up everything that happens to us. This work is based on responsibility. **You just torture yourself and make healing impossible by holding on to blame.**"

"Okay, okay, I've been there every time! I know this is something I need to work through and I will. Do you have any coffee? I'd like a cigarette, too." Richard was holding his breath.

"We have herbal teas, Richard, but no coffee. I suspect that your stress level may be elevating and perhaps caffeine and nicotine are ways you control your feelings. If you use those drugs to relieve stress and block Truth, chances are you are addicted to them. They support your illusions and projections and seem to protect you from your pain, but they function as anesthetics and are destructive to the *body*. I would suggest, since more feelings are surfacing, that you might let go of the need for a cigarette and coffee for the next hour or so and see if anything more comes up."

"I have noticed that I tend to smoke more when I'm upset but never understood why. I'll give it a try, I'll hold off smoking."

⊶ Key Thought—The bad news: You are the only problem in your life. The good news: You are the solution.

Notes

dr. michael ryce

10

ANCIENT WISDOM

Most people, once they have clarity about the cause of the pain in their lives, are excited and eager to go to work on taking care of issues which need to be resolved. Richard was the exception. When I spoke again of *True Forgiveness* being the solution, he went ballistic.

Richard's voice deepened. "Forgiveness!? Come on. I've been listening to your explanation but I've tried forgiveness; it changes nothing!" he bellowed.

"Take another deep breath," I suggested. "Remember I spoke of letting go of the dialogue in your head? I invite you to listen to my words, not your past realities about forgiveness and the negative associations you have made.

"The way forgiveness is commonly taught is only a shadow of its true meaning and function. In this culture, we've generally accepted a substitute for *True Forgiveness*. Due to our own ignorance we've bought into the common belief that forgiveness means 'letting them off the hook' for the terrible things *they* have done to us. This is a Greek concept. It comes from a mind-set that *externalized everything* and *attributed cause* to the *outside world*. This is not how *True Forgiveness* was originally presented and not even close to the original Aramaic concept!

"Engaging in *True Forgiveness* is required to heal. I personally believe that human beings and even civilizations cannot survive long term without it. Observe the direction our culture has been moving and I think you will see what I mean."

Richard seemed to be baiting me. "You've mentioned Aramaic several times, does it have something to do with religion? If so, I'm really not interested in hearing about it."

"The Aramaic language is an ancient tongue, spoken by the originators of at least five of the world's major religions. Religions address the topic of *Forgiveness*, of course, but the topic itself is not the exclusive property of the religious. We need not speak of *Forgiveness* in a religious context in order to experience its enormous practical value."

"For me," Richard began, "forgiveness has been linked to religion, something which doesn't interest me. It never occurred to me that it could be useful in a practical sense outside of the religious context." He softened a little as he continued, "Tell me more about this Aramaic and why it is so important."

"According to historians, the Aramaic language sprang to life fully matured. There was no developmental period nor any known place of origin, and Aramaic is one of the oldest spoken and written languages in the world. It was the language of the day throughout the Persian and Babylonian empires. From 1,000 BC to 1,000 AD, Aramaic could be heard from the Mediterranean to the Great Wall of China; it is still spoken today in some villages of Lebanon and in the mountains of northern Iraq.

"The Zoroastrian, Hebrew, Christian, Islamic and Baha'i faiths were all originally taught in Aramaic, and it is the language of many of the Dead Sea Scrolls. It was the native tongue of Moses, Abraham, Jesus, Mohammed and Baha'u'llah."

"How does that relate to my twentieth century mind?"

"The Aramaic language and culture impart a practical understanding of human behavior and clearly explain how the mind works. It has the ability to convey deep psychological meanings by simply adding prefixes and suffixes to root words, an ability unknown in any other language. It seems to me that it has this ability because the Aramaic peoples had an understanding that no other culture has acquired to date. This ancient language encompasses a technology desperately needed to heal the insanities in our culture.

"The level of comprehension of human function reflected in Aramaic is unknown in the West; and what today is thought of as religion was then simply guidance for daily living. It taught people how to best handle their family lives, relationships, sexuality, businesses, taxes, legal matters, land, crops, inheritance and finances. Unfortunately, its advice has been, for the most part, ignored and thought of as antiquated by the 'modern mind.' It has a thought structure so radically different from what most of us have been taught that, when first confronted, it shocks the Western mind."

"Still sounds like a religious spiel to me!" he exclaimed.

"Can you let go of the conversation in your head long enough to hear that there might be something more in the Scriptures than religion? If you investigate genuine Spiritual teachings you will find they are about life; they deserve serious consideration! In Truth, they are simply an owner's manual for your life, relationships and *body*."

"Okay! You've got my curiosity. What you have said so far makes sense, so I'll listen," came Richard's wary reply.

"Once you go beneath the misinterpretations and grasp the original Aramaic thought structure in the Scriptures, you might experience, as I have, a clarity that is profound. What today is called religion has its roots in solid, down-to-earth guidance. **The original intention of religion was to create a community where it was safe and nurturing to live differently than the insanity we humans have created in the world—a community that taught people how life worked and instructed people how to achieve the best life had to offer.** Many religions still hold fast to this as their goal.

"Do you recall hearing quotes from the Scriptures like, 'Do not judge by appearances,' 'Do not defile the temple' and 'The wages of sin is death'?"

"Yes, and it never made one lick of sense to me, either. When I was a kid, I heard hypocrites spouting that stuff all the time, then they would do the exact opposite when they thought no one was looking. It sure turned me off," Richard said with disgust.

"I hear it was confusing for you to see people not walking their talk. With the amount of energy and resistance you have around this conversation, I suspect you were abused due to their hypocrisy? Were you?"

"My folks talked about Love and honesty at church, but beat me up, verbally and physically, at home. If I spoke up or asked why they acted so differently in public, the beatings doubled. I had to lie to keep the family secrets. I had to be dishonest in order to make it look like everything was okay—or I'd be punished. Keeping up appearances was *demanded* of me. It was pretty crazy. While I was being lectured on the value of telling the Truth, I was *required* to live a lie!" Richard bit his nails as he replayed his story. The way he was sitting reminded me of a scared, angry, little boy, perched on the edge of his seat ready to escape.

"I saw hypocrisy in the minister and deacons—lots of people. *They* were always telling *me* I was a sinner. That was painful." As he finished his story, he was rigid and holding his breath.

"Take a breath, Richard. **Holding your breath is exactly how you acquire a past about something and carry it with you. Holding your breath attaches the pain of an experience to a reality in the mind. If that reality is triggered, even though external circumstances do not justify it, there will be pain.**

"Richard, has it occurred to you that just because someone could not live up to a teaching does not mean it has no value or that the problem lies within the teaching? It sounds like one of the issues was your parents' inability to live up to their ideals. That does not make them good or bad. It simply means that, like all humans, they were not perfect. It seems you attached the imperfection and abuse of your parents to their religion.

"Projecting your pain onto religion makes it difficult for you to see any benefit in it. I have seen many who simultaneously abandon their relationship with their parents and Spiritual support systems in this fashion."

"Hmm, I guess my parents deserve the right to be human, too. Perhaps I expected too much of them," he pondered, "I can see that they were trying—and doing the best they could. I feel relieved just knowing that."

"That insight is a result of *Forgiveness*. It's a small but significant example of how *Forgiveness* works," I said.

"What do you mean?"

"You had a reality, a 'file' so to speak, called 'My parent or parents should have been perfect.' According to your perception, they weren't, and you attached the pain, abuse and resentment you experienced with them to your mind's file on 'parents.' Whenever the reality 'parent' was triggered, your perception of them or yourself as a parent was clouded by the complex of thoughts and feelings in that file.

"In Aramaic, *Forgive* means to cancel. The minute you loosened your grip on your need for them to be perfect, in effect, **you canceled your need for that perfection**. The result of that action is your 'parent' file opened and the abuse, pain and resentment it contained began to release. This is *True Forgiveness* in Aramaic, certainly a radically different action than letting them off the hook. As the cloud over your perception of them lifted, a painful reality was in process of being forgiven and you can now see them more realistically."

With the release of the negativity, Richard's mind can now generate a more accurate image of and realities about his parents.

Stored negativity that darkens the glass of perception being released.

Parents

Dad

Mom

THE RESULT OF TRUE FORGIVENESS

"I'm not sure I heard everything you just said, but I sure feel relieved," Richard sighed.

"You are not the only one who will experience relief, Richard. This release will impact not only your mother and father but, due to the new clarity in your 'parent file,' your capacity to parent will also be enhanced.

"Notice your parents were not involved in this process and neither they nor the actualities of the past have changed, yet, you feel better. **You are always in charge of your feelings, and no change is required of anyone but you in order for you to heal! Our natural state is happiness. The human being is designed to feel good.** Just observe the ease and happiness of a child before it is impacted by our cultural insanities."

dr. michael ryce

"You said the release process *began,* michael. Does that mean it's not complete? Will I have to go through more of that pain?" Richard winced as he wrapped his arms around his knees.

"Healing is not an *event,* Richard, it is a process. It takes time and happens in stages. You will tend to experience your process as painful as long as you resist it and want to hold on."

"How long will it take?" he asked.

"As long as it takes. It can be a pleasant, exciting and easy experience, though. Unfortunately, many, because of resistance, don't go through it easily. It is an individual process that can be accelerated," I added.

"How?!"

"There are many factors that determine how quickly you move through your healing, how easily you process. These include your nutrition, exercise, your support system and a host of other factors. **The best way I know to accelerate healing is to apply what I like to call 'Cosmic Grease.' It is the willingness to embrace with Love whatever you find inside yourself. It speeds up process immeasurably.**"

> ⚿ KEY THOUGHT—Willingness is the "Cosmic Grease" that helps you move easily and quickly through your issues.

"I've heard of changing the past, is that what I've just done?"

"Your *Forgiveness* did not change the past, but it changed a reality in your mind *about the past*. There is no reason why the pain of old realities should be carried inside of us. Your relief and release is a good example of the successful use of *True Forgiveness*. It is wise to remember a success like this if resistance to change surfaces in the future. Give yourself a pat on the back. Go ahead, actually pat your back. It's more than a cliché. Intentionally emphasizing the positive effects of an action or attitude is known as a positive anchor. When you anchor things through this kind of emphasis, you will be more inclined to repeat them in the future."

"I'm kind of sensing what you're saying, michael, but it's a little overwhelming. I feel better, but I'm still confused. I don't know why. I'm not sure I quite understand what just happened." Richard leaned over and untied his shoes as he spoke. He stretched his legs out in front of him as he settled back into his seat. Even though he didn't understand everything we had covered, he looked more relaxed and comfortable. For the first time since he arrived, the lines in his forehead were softening.

"Richard, **as you undo old patterns, some confusion is normal**. Bringing your conflicting thoughts and feelings to the surface as you heal creates that kind of effect.

"Your relief in the situation with your parents came from spontaneous forgiveness, the kind that happens in an accidental and haphazard fashion. One of the primary tools we offer, which you can learn to use and take home with you, is called 'The Reality Management Worksheet.' The purpose for this tool is to teach, on an experiential level, how both joy and pain are created. It is a reliable, scientific method you can use at any time to let pain go and really embrace the joy."

"If what you're saying is true, I want it!" Richard exclaimed.

> ⚷ KEY THOUGHT—Willingness is the key to empowerment. If you want to be empowered, use the key.

11

PROCESSING AND GOING UNCONSCIOUS

It is quite common, as people begin to understand this work, for them to flip-flop between clarity and their old beliefs. This is to be expected as one learns a new conceptual language and a new way of thinking. Richard was no exception to this rule.

"I don't quite get it yet, but I am beginning to realize how easy it is to lapse into my old beliefs, and it doesn't feel very good," Richard said, frustrated with himself.

"I'm not quite sure what you mean," I replied.

"An hour ago, I grasped the idea that healing and responsibility are an 'inside job.' It was very clear to me then," he answered. "Now I've reverted to my old hostility, cynicism and blame. I'm sorry I jumped all over you about the Aramaic, michael."

"May I offer a different thought, Richard?" He nodded in agreement. "People who say 'I'm sorry' a lot usually end up being sorry people. In this work, we have an alternative to that. If you wish to apologize, go ahead, but drop the idea of being sorry. Replace it with a statement of what you intend to do if that situation arises in the future."

"I'm feeling a little lost. It's like I'm back where I started. I'm ready to jump whole hog into blame again and I don't understand how I lost the level of insight I had. I don't have any idea what you mean when you suggest I replace saying 'I'm sorry.'"

"It's natural at this stage, with two belief systems fighting for your attention, to waver in your clarity. You are doing just fine on that count. The alternative to 'I'm sorry' would sound something like, 'I apologize for taking out my hostility on you, michael. In the future, if anger and resistance come up in me, I will breathe and work toward taking responsibility for my upset.'"

Richard took a deep breath and released a long exhale. "I commit myself to being responsible for my feelings and breathing instead of attacking! This is so *simple*, why didn't I think of it?"

"Practice. All of these tools are simple, it's just a matter of retraining our minds to think differently. In the Aramaic thought system, this issue was addressed by the statement that 'we would be transformed by the renewal of our minds.'"

I acknowledged him and assured him that he was doing fine and that, as he practiced using the tools, it would get easier to hold to his new thought structure when old patterns kicked in. "When you become aware or conscious of your own behavior and the inclinations that come from your internal reality structure, you have made a giant leap. It usually takes much longer before someone can see the inconsistencies in their thoughts, words or behaviors. **We call a loss of awareness of one's internal processes *going unconscious*.** Catching yourself at that is a wonderful skill to develop."

"R-i-g-h-t," Richard groaned.

"Take my word for it," I offered reassuringly. "Catching yourself is a good thing, honest." In addition to the frustration of feeling like he was slipping back into old thinking patterns, he also had twenty questions begging to be answered—all at once. This happens as people get more involved in this study. It can be difficult to keep the issues and insights straight. Some circling through and around the questions that come up is inevitable.

64

"This work, with its synthesis of so many disciplines, is a lot of information to digest in one sitting! It takes patience and time to build the brain cells and integrate those disciplines so that the tools become fully available and functional. There is an intricate pattern of interconnectedness which one must usually step back to see. As you do your work and sit with the insights that come, you will see how all of life is synchronized. You might want to reread the first insight from *The Celestine Prophesy*," I suggested. Richard still looked a little bewildered and, once again, was holding his breath.

"Keep breathing, healing looks like this. When old trash surfaces it is not fun, but sorting through what comes up, in the presence of Love, is what clears it out. Can you remember feeling this lack of clarity ever before?" I asked.

"Why don't you just ask me about my whole life?" he said with annoyance. All of a sudden an impish grin came across his face. "I get it. Why should I expect to deal with everything in an instant when it has taken years to get to where I am today, right?"

"As I said, it is a process."

"Does this mean I have to go digging through and re-experiencing everything in my past? I don't want to do that."

"No, there is no digging around required. **If you get good at re-experiencing your past, that's what you'll be good at—re-experiencing your past.** The practice with these tools is to hold a space of Love within yourself and live in today's world from that perspective. If something less than Love surfaces at any time, use the tools. As you do this, things from your past that impact your present perceptions will surface to be healed. You can only deal with and heal your reality structure in the present. Are you breathing, Richard?"

"Breathing! Why do you keep bugging me about breathing? What's the big deal?!" Richard cried angrily.

"Hey, I'm on your side, remember? I'm here to support your healing. Recall when we spoke about how pain gets locked into a reality? **Holding your breath causes feelings and events to be linked and stored as a unit. The energy of an experience you are having is suppressed into tissue when the breath is held. Rather than staying stuck in upset, if you breathe, it is easier for old patterns to break lose and distasteful present moment experiences to pass.** The breath is the switch that either restricts or allows energy to move in your system. Keeping your breath open makes healing much easier."

> ⚷ KEY THOUGHT—Every day it's the same old thing. Breathe! Breathe! Breathe!

"That fits for me. I'm just now recalling that when I was a kid I was told over and over again that I was a sinner. I think that may have done more to drive me away from the church than the hypocrisy I saw. When you remind me to breathe, it feels like that old pain of being condemned," Richard shared.

"Let's process through what is happening and look at it, step by step," I suggested.

"Wait a minute, just what is 'processing'?" he asked.

"I've pretty much described it, but **processing is defined as the capacity to hold Love Conscious, Active and Present when something less than Love surfaces. It is the main key in healing; it releases the painful component of every reality unlike Love.** It is not an intellectual process, though the intellect can initiate it.

"Processing releases aliveness within. Once its energy starts to move in you, you can never be the same again. You are changed and transformed—forever. When it happens, it may be like a lightning bolt or a gentle breeze, it does not matter. Its stirrings are often unconscious at first. You may not know what has happened but you will know that *something* has occurred. Value it. Treasure it. It

dr. michael ryce

is the active power of Love *re-organ-izing* the core of your being and the expression of the cause of your existence.

"That makes sense and definitely sounds like something I want. Let's go ahead and see if I can process what just occurred." He looked intrigued.

"Your pain around taking on the 'sinner' label may have stemmed from your beliefs about being unjustly accused. We had recently discussed your having been called a sinner, so the idea of being unjustly accused was just beneath the surface in your mind.

"By repeatedly reminding you to breathe, that which was close to the surface was triggered. My reminders easily resonated your old feelings about being accused and doing something wrong. Remember, old suppressed realities distort perception. As a kid, you were probably told a thousand times that you were a 'sinner,' and each time your pain was reinforced. Your outburst about breathing was aimed at what triggered this old pain—my reminder to breathe. Your hidden agitation was expressed as unconscious behavior—an attack toward me. Recall your intention when you apologized to me earlier?"

"Yes, I am willing to be responsible for what I feel and I'll continue to breathe," he said with determination. As he looked at me, there was a warmth in his eyes I hadn't seen before. Ancient hurts were being transformed into Love. "I really appreciate your sticking with me through all of this, michael. A few minutes ago your reminder seemed like a hassle, now I feel grateful for it. I can see that a reminder to breathe and the surfacing of old agitation is an opportunity to heal the feelings I have about being called a sinner and being condemned; it is not a reason to attack."

Richard sighed heavily. "I wouldn't have guessed there were so many dynamics under the surface driving my behavior. Is that where unconsciousness comes from?"

"Unconsciousness and projection. Notice, the agitation you had was actually about being called a sinner, something that perhaps you have not heard in decades. Your old feelings were triggered by my reminder, and you projected your upset into your mind's image of me," I said.

"Hold on," Richard said, holding up his hand as if he were stopping traffic. "I think I'm understanding unconsciousness, but what you just said about projection went right over my head."

"Remember the physicists' point of view that everything is energy? The bottom line is that there is no physical world."

"Okay, but what does that have to do with projection?" Richard questioned.

"Everything. In Truth, the world is a whirling mass of energy, a sea of motion, with nothing solid. No 'thing' exists apart from that energy. The mind is what generates the image that 'things' are solid. The mind, because of its training, blocks the evidence that all things are connected and provides the illusory image that everything is separated. The *only* place a *body* exists is as an image in the mind.

"The suppressed energies you hold from an old experience, when triggered by someone, are used by your mind as the foundation of the image it generates of them. We cannot see a suppressed attribute someone triggers as our own because it shows up in our minds as belonging to them. We actually project our attribute into our brains' image of them. Ahh, the relief of successful projection! One problem remains, however! **Why am I in pain if it is *their* error? Why am I the one who is there every single time?**

"In the Aramaic Scriptures, this is the issue that was being referenced when they said, 'Beware you who judge another, for that in which you judge another, *you have been* guilty of *practicing.*' I think you'll find the Aramaic concept of sin will tie this all together in a way that makes sense. I invite you to notice how practical and informative these Aramaic ideas are when you see them in the context of real life."

68

"Here we go with sin again, michael. I don't know whether to love you or hate you. I feel inspired and overwhelmed at the same time. It seems like the more I hear of what you say, the more work I realize I have to do. Does it ever end?"

"I'm not sure when the end comes. Again, I remind you, it is a process. Your feeling overwhelmed is pretty much on track for where you are. Almost everyone cycles through this stage several times as they learn this work. The healing accelerates as you **develop the capacity to hold a space of Conscious, Active, Present Love while unresolved issues surface.**"

"Conscious... What?" Richard sputtered. "I can't even say it, let alone do it! What does that mean?"

"That is a key question and before we get into an emotionally loaded concept like sin, let's talk about the power of holding a space of Love and how to do it," I suggested.

> ⚷ KEY THOUGHT—Is remembering to use the tools and then using them a difficult way to live? No. What is truly difficult is living life without the tools.

Notes

dr. michael ryce

12

HOLDING
A SPACE OF LOVE

"The best exercise I know to practice and strengthen your ability to hold a space of Love is to close your eyes and allow your self to become quiet. With your awareness focused inside, think of that which inspires in you the clearest, strongest, most powerful Love you are capable of feeling... "

"What if I feel nothing?" he interrupted.

"In my workshops, Richard, I often ask the question, 'Do you remember a time when you looked at the way people around you lived their lives and asked yourself if things were supposed to work this way?' The majority of people answer a resounding 'Yes!' When quizzed further, virtually everyone says they remember knowing life was about Love, caring and support. Each then recounts how they cut themselves off from Love.

"Each generation of children is seduced into giving up their *experience* of a world based on Love. They exchange this for a world controlled through fear, anger and manipulation. They are often taught that this tradeoff is the only way to get 'things' and 'be successful' in the 'real' world. The ancient Aramaic teachings warned us to be careful that we do not allow ourselves to be 'conformed to this world.'

"Often, if we allow ourselves to fall into the world's ways we cut ourselves off from Love. It then feels like a void when we first attempt to return to the experience of Love, as we do in this exercise. If you continue to practice, over time, the experience of Love will grow.

"Once you feel Love, imagine yourself intensifying it until it fills every cell in your *body*. The next step is to open your eyes and imagine extending that Love out through your eyes to someone or to some situation in your world.

"Another step is to enfold yourself in that Love and, when possible, look in a mirror as you do. Invest some time in this exercise and soon you will find Conscious, Active, Present Love will become a part of your vocabulary and your life!"

When Richard first called me, he was on his way out West to start a new life. Now he asked if a simpler solution might not be to just move on. "After all," he thought aloud, "if there is no one to trigger the pain, life is fine."

For many people the geographic cure is an option, but it is only a temporary solution. The problem with the geographic cure is that we take ourselves and our whole reality structure with us and attract similar situations as a result. Running away does not work because the painful reality is carried within the person running. **The only *permanent solution* is to understand and heal what is at the root of the reality structure causing the pain. Holding a space of Love while the underlying reality surfaces is how we heal.**

> **⊙━╤ KEY THOUGHT**—The Commitment on the back of this book is a major key in the healing process. It is a set of tools that show how to develop a space of Love in relationships with self and others.

13

OFF THE MARK

"I invite you to focus on holding a space of Love for yourself as we talk about sin, Richard. Watch what surfaces and be aware of your present moment realities.

"Most of us have bought into sin as something terrible and awful. It is something we have been taught to feel guilty and bad about. Sin was originally meant to be positive feedback. The English translation of the Aramaic word, *khata,* is 'sin.' It is an archery term. When you fired at a target and missed the bull's eye, the scorekeeper yelled, 'Sin!' It meant, 'You are off the mark,' which, in practical terms, means improper for your energy system or less than your highest and best. It does not mean you are evil, damned or should be groveling in the dirt. The simple implication is to adjust your aim, it's time to take another shot, time to do something differently in your life!

"The human energy system is based on Love and created in the image and likeness of Love. When you put an energy that is less than what is proper into that system, you defile or destroy it. In the interest of self-preservation, it is good to have accurate feedback and know when you have sinned!!"

"That sure puts things in a different light," Richard said.

"Yes, and it is also interesting to see that the Aramaic understanding of life is reinforced and proven by the latest in physics. If we could ask Albert Einstein about the world we call physical, he would tell us it does not exist. He would tell us that matter is energy that *appears* as a solid.

"The Aramaic Scriptures refer to the world of 'appearances,' cautioning not to judge by them. If we think the world is physical, we have judged by its *appearance*—not the *fact of what it is.* Is it possible that the world is energy, void of solid form and organized into the *appearance of form*? If all is energy, the body—in Aramaic the 'temple'—is energy. Recall that relative to *every* energy system, there are basically two qualities: that which builds the system up, *integrative* energy, and that which burdens or tears the system down—*disintegrative* energy."

Richard grinned. "So, sin doesn't refer to me as a person? It is just information, just *feedback*? If someone of integrity told me I had sinned, he would simply be informing me of an error?"

"Yes. In ancient Aramaic times, if someone did not understand the intricacies of the human energy system, that person might go to a specialist for advice. That specialist would point out one's violations of the laws of the human energy system by calling them 'sins' and *invite healing*."

"It still feels like the old guilt trip. Or, how do you say it, michael? The reality of guilt is surfacing in my mind again?"

"That sounds like a more accurate and responsible way to say it, Richard. **Guilt is a human invention designed to change human behavior. Unfortunately, its effect is more often the reverse—it keeps people locked into their errors rather than prompting release from them.**

"Have you noticed that guilt usually precedes an act? It is an emotional energy that keeps error in the forefront of the mind. **People tend to be attracted to the behaviors that connect them to the most energy.** *Programmed* guilt perpetuates behaviors that *seem* to 'cause' guilt."

"You mean that guilt causes the behavior rather than the behavior causing the guilt?!" He seemed shocked by the idea. "Are you saying that guilt is purposely instilled to control people?"

"Perhaps. A false 'specialist,' one who didn't know any better or wanted to control those who consult him, might connect sin with 'guilt, bad and wrong,' and use those energies to bind someone to servitude. **Guilt is a connection in a mind between error and self-condemnation for that error.** The specialist with integrity would use the same opportunity, the same 'sin,' to teach the inquiring mind how to forgive and release itself from its errors, its guilt and 'sins.'

"It would be accurate to call the integrative form of energy 'holy,' rooted in the word whole, that which supports or builds the human system. The disintegrative, we might call 'evil.' Evil is 'bisha' in Aramaic and is another archery term. Sin is missing the bull's eye, and evil means 'off target,' missing the target altogether.

"An evil life in Aramaic is a life where one continuously engages in disintegrative energies—thus defiling one's own temple—creating dis-ease and self-destruction. In Aramaic, there was no moral component to the instruction, *'Stay away from an 'evil' person.'* It was pure pragmatism. If you associate with those who engage in disintegrative, self-destructive, 'evil' acts, their actions will soon appear normal. Making a behavior appear normal is the first step in persuading others to do the same."

Richard looked relieved. "When I was a kid, they always threatened me with death because I had sinned. What about that part of the Bible?"

"The reason you were told about sin in a threatening way was projection. Those who promote that type of interpretation are caught in their own *sin—fear*. **Fear clouds the minds and destroys the bodies of those who engage in it. That is why in the Aramaic Scriptures we were told that the *First Law* was Love.**

"In the Aramaic understanding, the Law and *its* Prophets *hang upon the condition of Love* in a mind, not on fear which produces unconsciousness and error. Without the condition of Love continuously present, the searching mind will project its own errors into what it studies and whatever or whomever it sees.

"*Only* a mind connected to Love has healed its capacity to project and can hold a true Spiritual perspective on life—only that mind can understand the Law and the Prophets. *All* others will distort their mind's view of the Scriptures by projecting their own pain, fear, hate and/or rage in to them. This produces a mind so insane that it can conceive of punishment, torture, and murder in the name Love as a 'logical,' 'reasonable' and 'holy' thing to do.

"Richard, 'the wages of sin is death' loses its threatening component when it is translated into the Aramaic language. It is not even a religious concept. It is a statement of simple physiology and a caution to be aware of the energies in which you engage. When you focus on energies that are inappropriate to your health, prosperity and wholeness you are living in 'sin.' Bring enough disintegrative energy into any system and it will fall apart and 'die.' The result of error is self-destruction.

"In Aramaic, energies of hate, fear, anger, envy, guilt, jealousy and the like are understood to be dis-integrative. They defile, or violate, the integrity of the 'temple' and eventually produce death in the person who engages in them. If you entertain those energies in your mind—no matter how justified you may seem—*you* are the one who receives the original of that destructive energy, the person you project it on gets only a carbon copy. That is what the Scriptures were attempting to teach.

> ⌖ KEY THOUGHT—The vessel in which negativity is stored *always* suffers more damage than the object upon which that negativity is poured.

"The world," I offered, "didn't get the message. The way fear is promoted in the media and in the world is almost like worship. Twenty-four hours a day, seven days a week we can tune into an information system that gives us the details, from anywhere on the planet, of the most terrible acts of humanity. It could be construed that fear has been purposely used to keep people in confusion, fear and overwhelm in order to control them."

Richard was engrossed in his thoughts. "It is almost like I've kept myself in prison by living in ignorance of this and allowing myself to be indoctrinated by fear and manipulation. It's a pretty sobering thought to realize I have been a manipulator and have purposely used that tactic by inspiring fear in people with whom I live. From what I had been taught, it seemed like a normal way to act.

"I see why it is important to be informed about these issues and why it is beneficial to be able to distinguish between integrative and disintegrative energies. I'm beginning to understand that we are responsible for what we set up in life."

"Exactly, Richard. In the Aramaic, fear was not promoted nor worshipped. It was treated as a 'demon' and 'cast out,' it was Forgiven. To emphasize condemnation, and abuse and batter people with fear, rather than encourage the expression and experience of Love and the Forgiveness of fear is error—sin. It is a signal that a person does not understand the Aramaic teaching nor the effects of a particular behavior on their own physiology. He or she does not understand how focusing on disintegrative energy produces dis-ease in *themselves*.

"Threat, fear, guilt, manipulation, confusion and overwhelm are dis-integrative energies that are at the root of most dis-ease processes. **The fact that there is a time delay between engaging in destructive behavior and the dis-eases that are sure to follow, hides the cause-effect relationship between the two.** It is then easy to blame our dis-eases on outside forces like bacteria, viruses and the like. More blame and projection."

"I can hear myself making excuses for my diseases, 'I caught the latest bug, it couldn't possibly be anything I have done!'" Richard reflected, tongue in cheek.

> ☞ KEY THOUGHT—It is your mind energy that is responsible for the condition of the tissue in your *body*. Louis Pasteur's final conclusion on disease: *The germ is nothing, the terrain is all!*

"Seriously though, I think I'm really starting to hear what you're saying," he said as he paused and contemplated how to put his new found insights into words. "See if this fits. I'm the one who has been there every time I've experienced anger, fear or guilt. I cannot feel those things unless they are inside of me and, if they are there, they are a burden to my system. They are *my* dis-ease!" As he spoke his hands were as animated as his face. He was obviously delighted with the depth of his understanding.

The man sitting beside me now looked much lighter and more relaxed than the one who arrived earlier in the day. "The way you present Spiritual teachings, michael, makes them sound simple, straightforward and workable. They seem almost necessary to life," he said with surprise. "It never occurred to me that Spirituality was so fundamental to living. I rejected Spirituality and religion totally due to the bitterness of my early experiences.

"It seems like I've been carrying the burden of rejecting my religion for an eternity. No wonder I'm exhausted. For years, without knowing what I was doing, I've been hiding a lot of pain from myself as I bought into the label of 'sinner.' It sounds like it's time for me to forgive my distorted realities about religion." The sincerity in Richard's voice indicated to me that a profound shift was happening for him, perhaps the most important of his life.

> ☞ KEY THOUGHT—Truth is always safe. Not sometimes, not most of the time, but all the time.

dr. michael ryce

14

CHOOSING TEACHERS

"There are so many people, Richard, who have rejected one of the most vital parts of their lives—their Spirituality. My observation is that those who do this are usually people who have listened to someone with no practical Spiritual savvy. Years of study and intellectual 'knowledge' about doctrine or religion does not necessarily mean one has any actual *Spiritual experience.*

"Translations of the Aramaic teachings are so distorted today," I said, "I often wonder if it has been done purposely." I felt some of my own upset at the thought. "The translations *appear* sound, but are twisted just enough to cover up the wisdom that was available through the original words.

"I am always amazed by people who have studied Greek interpretations, often called translations, of Aramaic teachings yet have no interest in the actual meanings of what they have studied. Without access to the originally intended meanings, which can *only* be understood through a comprehension of the conceptual framework of the Aramaic mind, it is difficult for people to apply the tools that were originally taught. Sound teachings have gone from being practical and down-to-earth tools to being impractical and unattainable. As a result, people miss out on the knowledge, understanding, healing benefits and comfort provided by the original teachings."

"Why would the teachings be distorted?" Richard inquired.

"There are three possibilities I see. One is that the expression of the ideas could have been limited by the ability of the language into which they were 'translated.' Recall the two-dimensional creature we talked about earlier had no words to express the Truth about the three-dimensional world? A language can only express understanding for which it has words.

"A second possibility is the level of understanding of translators who had little or no actual experience with the transforming power of the teachings. Without realizing it, they watered down this powerful ancient wisdom to their limited capacity. Can you possibly translate something beyond your level of comprehension?"

"I'm not sure what you are saying, michael."

"Let's use an example. Would you want to go to a chemistry lab and perform a complex and dangerous experiment on the instructions of a first year chemistry student who doesn't even know the language of higher chemistry?"

"Of course not, I would want a competent, experienced instructor who KNOWS. I would at least want the input of someone who had actually performed the experiment *and had it work*," came his emphatic reply.

"Would it be wise to demand the same from the person you choose to assist in your Spiritual process? Would it be equally wise to qualify the person who helps you reach a conclusion about whether such a thing as the Spiritual dimension even exists? Many have never thought of consciously choosing their Spiritual leaders, or considered what the appropriate criteria are for making that choice.

"There are voices in the world that scream, 'There is no Spiritual life!' and 'All religion is a hoax!' It amazes me how many people unthinkingly follow the advice of those voices. Have you ever asked yourself what qualifies them to give you advice? I find the fact that people listen to these voices especially shocking, when

I consider that the majority of those advisors are screaming out of their own pain, which tends to render them unconscious. Many tend to listen to those voices and, in succeeding years, when the words of the unqualified echo in their heads, they mistake those thoughts as their own.

"I have never heard anyone who has had a Spiritual experience say such things as 'hoax' or 'there is no Spiritual life.' I have also observed many who have said such things change their minds very quickly when they have an *actual* Spiritual experience."

"Hmmm. What is the third cause you have in mind when you spoke of reasons for distortion, michael?"

"The third possibility I see is that the teachings were purposely falsified to mislead and control people."

"I see why there is so much conflict, confusion and infighting among Spiritual groups. It sounds like each of us has to take responsibility for our own process, clean up our own mind and choose our teachers wisely." Richard appeared to feel safe enough to explore more about his Spirituality. "As a young man, I dumped all involvement with anything that smacked of Spiritual content as a result of my religious upbringing. I also fell into thinking *things* would make me happy. Now I'm seeing that no matter how much I have, if I don't work out what is in my own head, possessions alone won't satisfy me or bring me peace, happiness and security."

I agreed. "Things can be nice to have. They can bring comfort, but comfort does not heal," I offered. ***"Only* with tools *designed* to complete the task, can we heal our pain.**

"It seems like seeking out tools is the sensible thing to do. Spirituality has always been the place where healing tools are found. Religious movements based on Spiritual experiences sometimes carry through with that purpose and sometimes go in the opposite direction and attempt to control people by inflicting pain rather than healing it. **Where you go for Spiritual advice is important.**

"It is interesting to note that people who take the advice of only the best lawyers, who travel the world in search of the top physicians, who want only the soundest of financial advisers, will accept the opinions of those with little or no experience when it comes to Spiritual matters. Does that make sense when making decisions that could have long-term consequences?"

Richard agreed that confusion is rampant in Spiritual circles. "Where can I go to learn how to make such decisions, michael?"

"It helps to build some brain cells about the ways Spiritual teachings are used in our culture. I think you will find that will clarify the process of choosing."

☑ Two Spiritual Teachers:

"1. True Spiritual teachers use Spiritual teachings to liberate people from their pain and the habits which produce pain and suffering. This style of teaching comes from those who inspire and motivate others by example. They have Spiritual experience and are accomplished in that realm. The fruit, or result, of these teachers' work is a shift from the insanity, hatred and what I like to call *little violences* of the world *to peace, harmony,* and *abundance.* These teachers, while not perfect, focus on their own work. Their hand is always out, compassionately extended for the purpose of supporting anyone who is healing.

"2. False teachers use Spiritual teaching deviously. Under the guise of a promise to save or liberate people from present or future pain and suffering, they use threat and fear tactics to drive people deeper into their trauma. Often suffering is promoted as good and necessary and the promise of liberation applies to some sort of an afterlife, which cannot be proven nor disproven. These 'teachers' also have a hand out, but it is gathering for themselves or their organizations and using some form of threat or fear tactic to keep people in tow.

"The false teacher uses religion to acquire political, financial and/or behavioral control over people. The incentive for the weak or insecure to enter this type of religious order and join the ranks of false teachers is evident. A disproportionate percentage of the assets, power, sexual favors and money of the people they control and manage accrues to them."

"Sounds like pretty heavy condemnation, michael. I thought this work was supposed to be positive in its thinking. I don't know if I want to hear this," Richard chided.

"I understand where you are coming from, Richard. If you were in a prison, and did not know it, wouldn't you need to understand something about its structure in order to find your way out? If, from within your prison walls, you said to me, 'michael, I'm a positive thinker. Don't tell me I'm in prison or how I got here. Just show me out.' Wouldn't it be foolish to lead you to the high fence, knowing you'd be stuck there without a ladder?

"If you had allowed the space for me to tell you about the high fence beforehand, you could have gotten the ladder from the basement in advance. Knowing what we're dealing with can be practical help to us. Planning ahead and being prepared for what we will encounter is sometimes more important than all the positive thinking the world has to offer.

"Showing up at the fence without a ladder is doing life the hard way. I'm here to support you in making life easy and joyful—meeting your challenges with the practical tools and knowledge you need. I support you in meeting the obstacles in life with ladder in hand—that is, living life from an empowered state."

"I'm willing to have that support and have life be easier. I'm just not clear yet about how this fits in with being a positive thinker. I've always been told I should be more positive, and I've been working on that," Richard confided.

"This work is not about being a positive thinker, that can get you into a lot of trouble!" I offered.

"What are you talking about, michael?! My friend, who insisted I call you, said the work you have developed is the ultimate in positive thinking!"

"This work is about honest and appropriate thinking, Richard. There is a disorder that I call 'Premature Positive Thinking.' If you have a negative foundation and refuse to deal with it, positive thinking is very appealing. It becomes another way to avoid. There is a benefit to positive thinking—life improves.

"The problem, as I've observed it, is that the Premature Positive Thinker has to be on top of 'things' all the time. The stress of keeping the negative down with a positive attitude means there is never a minute's rest. Premature Positive Thinking can lead to becoming like the type 'A' personality. It can result in overload and, if you let up the positive thinking for even one moment, things start to crash; the benefits disappear and you get to start over. It's a difficult way to live.

> ☞ KEY THOUGHT—This work is not about premature positive thinking. It is about honest, appropriate thinking and holding yourself and others accountable for all behaviors.

"Premature Positive Thinking also produces dis-ease. Appropriate and honest thinking is the goal. The only healing and truly restorative processes are those which allow stored negativity to be surfaced, exposed to Love, and released.

"Let go of the need to build a positive framework on top of a negative foundation. Acquire tools and deal with the negative as you develop the capacity to naturally and gracefully live from the positive. In this system, there is no stress from 'trying' to keep a falsehood in place. There is no pretentious thinking because everything less than the positive is given space to surface and heal.

In the short term, it takes extra work and commitment to do what I am suggesting, but in the long run it leads to a much easier life.

"With these tools, the *body*, rid of its burdens, can then use its own recuperative powers to rebuild. **Dis-ease is not natural.** Health is our natural state and is always possible when interference is removed. True health is impossible to achieve when discord is present. This understanding is the foundation of any true health care system. Without this deeper comprehension of healing any system of 'healing' is bound to be a 'disease care' system which will consume enormous amounts of wealth."

"That fits for me, but I'm still not sure," Richard looked at me quizzically as he spoke. "Isn't it positive thinking to want to Love everyone and let go of my need to condemn? It seems like you're telling me not to think that, but if I don't I'm stuck with my negative thinking—being angry and blaming others."

"Let me go back to the prison analogy and clarify my point about condemnation. I don't have to condemn the prison in order to inform you of its structure or to say, 'Here are the pitfalls, this is where the guards are and the lowest part of the fence is over there. You will need a ladder and a positive sense of yourself and what you will face in order to make it through.'

"I can say, 'Beware, the earmarks of the false teacher are_____' and identify their characteristics. I can let you know that certain behavior does not support your highest and best. I can warn you, 'Be aware if you find yourself or someone else doing these things,' and be in support of healing those behaviors—all without condemning. However, if your inner dialogue speaks to you frightfully about condemning, perhaps you will need to heal your listening, and rid yourself of the need to gloss over what does not work.

"There are two different issues here, Richard. **One is condemning, the other is identifying.** If you never make the distinction between the two, you will be vulnerable to either engaging in, or being taken in by the thinking of the false teacher.

When we support destructive behavior in the world we are engaging in disintegrative energy.

"False teachers operate in religion, business, government, media, education and families. They can show up anywhere. As we develop the brain cells, we can see the behavior for what it is. If there is condemnation in us, we can then take responsibility for that condemnation, heal it and bring healing and insight to false teachers. The alternative is to refuse to identify what is happening and not know why there is pain, rage or suffering.

"It is amazing how many people are continuously angry—you know, the type who slam doors, kick the cat and beat their kids—and they cannot identify the source of their anger. Most often the rage comes from the helplessness of being in the grips of the false teacher and not knowing how to take back one's own power. **The refusal to learn and live in harmony with Truth leads to destructive behavior. The abused become manipulators and abuse those who are weaker, and this serves as a substitute for the power one is lacking over one's own life and is a compensation for insecurity.**"

"I've felt powerless most of my life, michael. I feel I've been controlled through my fear, and I usually respond with anger. I think you've got me pegged."

"Richard, it's an almost universal story. I could probably say the same thing to ninety percent of the population and be accurate. Most human beings have bought into reality structures, usually for security reasons, that allow them to engage in, support or be controlled by manipulative behavior and they unknowingly give up their aliveness to do it. With awareness of what is driving us and tools with which to heal, we can free ourselves from these patterned responses. It is important to be discriminating about what you serve with your intelligence, resources and time. **Right livelihood** means you do nothing that supports dis-integrative energy in the world and use your time, intelligence, money and energy to support only awareness and aliveness!

86

"The need to condemn negative behavior or those practicing it can also be healed. A willingness to investigate is required. Knowledge is power. Ignorance does not lead to healing, it leads to staying stuck behind the prison fence, suffering and pretending there is no way out—classic victimhood.

"With information, understanding and dedication, it is possible to create a space of healing for anyone who engages in negative behavior. This includes ourselves and *anyone* who takes advantage of another. With this understanding, we can also support the healing of people who set themselves up to be manipulated. Every player in a situation must be healed for a total shift to occur. Healing also means that each person involved automatically moves closer to the awareness of their true purpose and finds it easier to be guided in its accomplishment.

"It is valuable to comprehend the healing dynamic so that we have the capacity to choose what to do and what not to do. Understanding manipulation in no way evaluates what another has done or should do, for that is his or her business, not ours. However, having proper understanding allows the space for us to be held accountable and to hold others accountable for what is done.

"This brings us to another belief promoted by the manipulator: 'You are bad and wrong if you ever catch me at my game or try to hold me accountable.' There are people functioning out of their pain who manipulate and engage in actions you want to avoid. Their actions and cover stories can be very subtle; some have spent their whole lives building a camouflage for their manipulations.

"It is important, especially since most of us were born into a manipulative world, to understand the subtleties of manipulation. Like the fish that cannot see water because it is so close, some forms of manipulative behavior are so ingrained, they are invisible. I have observed that often, a person being abused thinks it is normal and appropriate to be treated that way.

"When an *abuser* is confronted, their response is usually, 'That's not abuse, that is proper behavior.' Recall the waitress, Richard? When you became conscious of your behavior, you categorized it as 'destroying.' Prior to having the brain cells to see it for what it was, didn't you see it as proper? Remember, you were *just protecting yourself.* That 'protection' was manipulation. **The ability to identify conduct for what it is, is important in breaking through the automatic cycles of behavior.**

"When people who need their daily dose of abuse are confronted, their response is usually the familiar, 'I thought that was the way it was supposed to be.' Their self-put-downs are cradled in guilt and the haunting thought that they deserve to be abused."

Richard listened attentively and appeared to absorb each idea. "This is such shocking information. The part of this that is hard to believe is how oblivious I have been to it all my life. I guess you could say I've been like the person in prison who thought that's just the way life is."

"We have all to some degree been trained in the fear of the world. Each of us, to some extent, has been seduced by and engaged in manipulative behavior. Perhaps that is why most people would rather not admit, talk about and acknowledge the fact that they intimidate others. They do not face themselves as you are now."

Richard was on the edge of emotions surfacing but could not quite let go. Seeing the pained look on his face, I added, "I acknowledge your courage and your willingness to hear new information. That can be an especially difficult task when it involves looking at our own errors or the errors of the people we Love. It can be even more difficult when we start to let go of the parts of us that need to be released and healed."

> ⚷ KEY THOUGHT—It requires courage to look at ourselves. Having tools makes looking easier and more productive.

15

TRANSITIONS

"I'm not sure what you mean when you say letting go of the parts of us that need to heal, it sounds like I might lose something in the process," Richard confided.

"It is frightening to most people. For some, at first, it appears to be the down side to doing this work. As you engage in this type of thinking and heal, you will lose a very dear friend!"

"How so?" He looked puzzled.

"When you engage in *True Forgiveness*—fear, manipulation, blame and guilt are going to evaporate from your life. You'll no longer be able to play the role of victim, which has been a part of your life for so long. That friend is going to have to go."

"That's true," he admitted. "I am just now realizing how much of my life and identity have been tied up with guilt and fear. It does feel like a big part of me is going to disappear," he lamented. "I won't know how to act anymore. Who will I be?"

"Sounds like a part of you is already feeling sadness about the loss of those old personality roles you loved to play. Giving up old identities and roles is important in this work. Sometimes, those old 'selves' don't go without a fight and a struggle. The feelings of loss can be so strong they might feel like death.

"In Aramaic it was said that in order to live you had to die. This may sound like a ridiculous statement, but when you see that the old self—the false, disempowering self—has to go, or die, for the true self to live, it makes perfect sense because it is a death of sorts.

"Richard, it might help to notice that blame and victimhood deliver no benefits. Aside from a perverse sense of righteousness, martyrdom, or negative attention, did they ever bring any actual Love, benefit or reward?"

"That's an interesting question," Richard replied pensively. "I didn't realize how I distorted myself nor how twisted it is to take pleasure in being a victim. It seemed like a good way to get attention and not have to accept blame for anything. No matter what went wrong, I convinced myself it was always someone else's fault."

As he continued, I was aware of his efforts to keep breathing and sent a silent acknowledgment. "Another thing that seemed like a benefit at the time was that I pulled in sympathizers to listen to my stories and agree with me. It was a way to feel powerful. By manipulating others into being on my side, I rallied support against a common enemy, convincing myself and almost everyone else that I was right. I had all those people in the palm of my hand, agreeing with me as I attacked someone who was innocent.

"You said earlier, michael, that we never do to someone else what we have not already done to ourselves. I'm also realizing that we first have to create abuse within ourselves in order to abuse another or have another abuse us. I was trying to ostracize the person I blamed, but I was the one who ended up alone. In the end, my behavior led to nothing but gossip and lost friendships. I didn't even see my part in it.

"All I received for my efforts was negative attention and the same painful experiences over and over. When I was in the blame and guilt mode, it seemed like I had the power. Now, it looks more like a false, useless kind of control.

90

"My whole life I've loved delivering the line, 'You'll be sorry when you see what you have done to me!' I remember my dad saying it to my mom and my mom saying it to my sister. It's strange, but as I think of that, I feel a lot of sadness. I can see that I've followed the family relationship pattern. I've wanted to appear to be right and stay in control. By doing this, I was able to avoid dealing with my sadness."

I broke into his train of thought. "Richard, the need to control, as with violence and gossip, usually comes from insecurity. Guilt and blame are not really crutches that assist your life but rather a ball and chain that hold you back. They are energies that are 'off the mark.' Earlier, when we were talking about your mom, we established that people felt driven away by you. When those people left, you felt like the victim. **You are only a victim of the results of your own behaviors.**"

The insights Richard gleaned from doing his work were the fruit of his willingness to look at his own painful realities and would change his life forever. He was experiencing, first hand, that it was safe and healing to face himself. The change in him was visible. His posture became straighter and his voice deepened. He was in transition from victimhood to empowerment.

> ☐➔ KEY THOUGHT—Give yourself the opportunity to think new thoughts and test out the new behaviors that will come about as a result.

Notes

dr. michael ryce

16

HEALING
ABUSE AND VICTIMHOOD

"It's clear to me now that I set myself up. Strange as it sounds, I was comfortable in the role of a victim; I've practiced it all my life. I didn't realize I caused the trauma that was my constant companion," Richard volunteered.

"It seemed to benefit me to show how wounded I was, how much of a victim I was, because people didn't tend to hold me accountable. It seemed to save me from further punishment and put me in control. I can see, however, the first step in the process of becoming a 'victim' was my choice to be 'victimized.'

> ☞ KEY THOUGHT—There are no victims, only volunteers. We volunteer with the realities we hold.

"As I look at it, I can see I purposely played the victim role to keep people from victimizing me! What manipulation, what a twisted way I've used people," he mumbled to himself. "As I think about it, I fed on the energy of fear. It was that and anger. They seemed to be my only two choices. I really have some work to do if I'm going to change the foundation of my relationships from fear and anger to Love.

"I believe Love is the most powerful force on earth. It seems one of the benefits of giving up blame and guilt and letting go of my ball and chain is regaining my power. Is that it? Does this mean the choices I make are the key?" he asked hopefully.

"That's right, and the new choices you've been making today are grounding you in your power," I offered.

"Then you're saying that the power I lost playing the victim becomes available for me to consciously recreate my life? **To think about every part of me being aligned with and creating out of Love is pretty exciting stuff!**" he exclaimed.

"Yes, and it takes work. It is not an event that happens in a single moment, but a process that results from being responsible for what you set up in life. **Notice that the Truth is safe and healing.** Now that you are aware of behavior patterns that don't serve you, you are in a position to change them. *That's empowerment!*

> KEY THOUGHT—When you choose to be aware of behavior patterns that don't serve you, you are in a position to change them. *That's empowerment!*

"It sounds like the only way you thought you could step into your power, other than through victimhood, was through hostility."

"That is exactly what I thought. Without my anger, I was powerless," Richard confided.

"Hostility is one of the most addictive, damaging drugs there is. Every person who engages in it *needs their fix* to keep their pain suppressed. Those who use this drug encourage others to do the same because they themselves have not faced what they have suppressed with their *own* anger. Often, the rationalization that we have a 'right' to our anger is used to justify holding on to this form of self-abuse. We must be willing to deal with what we have hidden from ourselves and stop using that drug if healing is to occur."

"What are you talking about?"

"Do drugs suppress pain?" He nodded. "If you look at someone who is extremely hostile, you will always find deep emotional pain. Hostility sets up *body* chemistry that suppresses pain. Using hostility is like using any other drug. If one stops using their addictive substance, in this case the internal chemistry produced by hostility, they will go into withdrawal when the pain the drug has suppressed surfaces. That is the point at which the craving gets so strong many return to their supplier for another fix.

"One of the biggest challenges for the hostility addict is that the supplier is internal, a tricky pusher from which to break contact. Hostility must be treated like any other drug—**its use must stop**—if one is determined to recover. The other challenge is that society is the enabler."

Richard coughed. "What do you mean, enabler? What's that?"

"In traditional drug and alcohol treatment, the enabler is the person who supports the user by covering for or assisting him or her in keeping up the habit. For example, a husband who drinks to oblivion *every* weekend doesn't have to deal with his poor performance at work if his wife calls his boss and makes excuses for him. If he were required to face his boss and admit he had a hangover, he would have to deal with the consequences of his behavior. He might get fired if his boss knew what was going on."

He scowled. "If she didn't cover for him, there would be no paycheck and her family would starve."

"That's a great rationalization, the one most people use to avoid facing their problems. They justify addictive behavior and tolerate it as necessary because of thoughts like that. I invite you to interview a woman who has been there. If you could establish the cost to her mental, physical and emotional health, the strain on her children and other aspects of her life, it would be enormous. The impact of the anguish would be incalculable—hardly worth a paycheck. People deserve to live in gentle, Loving environments where aliveness, delight and joy are the norm. Anything less is an insult to the human spirit. With tools, it is possible for every person to create such a life."

> ○━┳ KEY THOUGHT—People deserve to live in gentle, Loving environments where aliveness, delight and joy are the norm. Anything less is an insult to the human spirit.

"I see what enabling is and I'm getting the idea that life can be different, but I don't understand what it means when you say society becomes the enabler."

"Any system that is set up to make it appear that abusive behavior is acceptable, desirable or necessary enables people who engage in that behavior to continue. People often support abuse in the world without realizing there is any option, that there is anything they can do about it. They don't speak up, similar to your experience as a kid where you kept the family secrets.

"Like the woman who continues to accept the abuse of an alcoholic husband in order to maintain her lifestyle, society rationalizes that the behavior of the hostility addict is required to maintain itself. The question, 'Do we need hostile behavior to maintain our society?' is an incorrect question. Hostility *is* an integral part of our current culture. The real question we should be asking is: 'Is that aspect of 'civilization' which requires violence worth perpetuating?'"

"How does society enable hostile people?"

"Richard, think of the functions and jobs that exist in our culture that support hostility as a normal and acceptable behavior; often the bully is not just tolerated, but welcomed. Many bureaucracies are fueled by hostility; in excess of fifty percent of the national budget is used to fund our war-making capabilities.

How many of these activities do you suppose are patterned after the abuse many people learned in childhood?"

"Probably the majority. How did those patterns begin for most people?" Richard asked.

"Many children are raised in homes where being beat up verbally, physically and emotionally is normal. They presume maltreatment to be a part of life. They usually hate the abuse and their abusers, but people tend to become what they hate. They then contribute to the society which, in turn, accommodates them by creating ways that they can earn a living by being abusive, thus maintaining those patterns set in childhood. By this action, society fulfills the role of the enabler and the cycle is passed on to the next generation. The mistreated, who are now in control, tend to become abusers themselves. Abuse does not become sane because it is institutionalized, accepted or looks normal."

"Well, it is necessary to fight back and protect yourself," he said in an argumentative tone.

"It is participation in that kind of thinking that is causing violence to become the norm in our culture. People tend to be so close to what they do, they cannot see their own insanity. Be assured that from within the society ruled by the 'volcano gods,' sacrificing a young maiden now and then was not bizarre. Torturing and burning people at the stake was not strange from within the belief system of the Inquisitors—it was a 'reasonable' way to save souls. **Reason, when not consciously governed, can justify *anything it can conceive of, anything it decides to do.***

"We live in a world where murder, war and violence are justified and condoned. Verbal, emotional and physical abuses are considered standard in many relationships and family systems. Parents lash out at children; teachers think it reasonable, in the name of 'discipline,' to verbally abuse, attack and put down the children they are 'teaching.' A child who kills is no longer an uncommon phenomenon.

"The media regularly portray 'little violences' as acceptable. Family members at each other's throats—attack, sarcasm and put-downs are presented as witty, normal, human interaction. Ever wonder why the divorce rate is so high? Healthy relationships are seldom represented or modeled anywhere in our world or media."

"Where have I been all my life?" He said, as he fumbled for words. "I've never thought about how previous generations or the media impact us. It never occurred to me that the world could be any different. I've never conceived that my hostility supports and contributes to the dynamic of violence in the world."

"Look around, you are not alone, Richard. These little violences rarely strike the sensibilities of anyone who has been trained to think of these forms of insult to human integrity as 'funny' and acceptable. From within the monumental violence of the way our world works, 'little violences' are seen as meaningless. I believe they are the tributaries that join to produce the destructive river of violence so prevalent in our world culture.

"In my experience, the reason for monumental violence is that many learn violence from conception—violence in thought, word and action. Its harmful nature in the family has, to a great degree, been ignored, though it is the beginning point of all conflict, divorce, murder and war. Children and adults are so confused as to what is reasonable, they often do not know when they are abusing others, being abused or abusing themselves. The end of this insanity on our planet begins when each of us acquires and uses the tools to heal the violence we do to ourselves and others. **Peace is not an objective, it is the pathway to sanity and healing.**"

> ⌕ KEY THOUGHT—The tools used to produce a result always produce a result like the tools.

"Fear and violence have been with us for all of history, michael. I want to live in peace as much as the next guy, but do you honestly think you can eliminate our world's insanities with these tools? Sounds like an impossible dream."

"Do you believe fear is a natural thing for us as human beings?" Richard agreed. "I think we've bought into a lie. **I believe it is time for us to confront the lie and face ourselves! It is time to heal the structures that support mental, emotional, spiritual, verbal and physical abuse. Hostility and violence in every form, within families, communities and nations, must come to an end if we humans are to survive, let alone live in peace.** Taking responsibility for one's own hostility and refusing 'the fix' each time the mind automatically offers it is one of the keys to healing and aliveness.

"A shocking belief held by many people is that peace is not possible nor is it desirable, and that violence is not only natural but necessary! It is a mind unwilling to be responsible, deal with its hurts and heal that promotes such an insane and barbaric dogma. That 'peace is not possible' is a rationalization for violence used by those who cannot or will not control their own thoughts, words or actions. I recall my son at about age eight asking, 'Why are people killed to show that killing people is wrong?'

> ⚯ KEY THOUGHT—Einstein said that you cannot solve a problem with the same mind that created it. The hostile mind is insane and *cannot* solve its problems. They can *only* be solved with the mind-set of Love.

"Let us have the courage to recover our lives and do the unthinkable: Question everything."

Richard and I decided to stretch our legs by taking a walk to the lake. A brisk walk up the hill left us both puffing but refreshed by the clean Ozark air.

Notes

17

THE BODY HAS A MIND OF ITS OWN

When we returned from our walk, the focus of our discussion turned to resonance and the mind. I explained that **the *Law of Resonance* is a law that governs all energy fields and is the law of energy exchange.**

"What is resonance?" Richard asked.

"Imagine I hold up a middle 'C' tuning fork and bring a second, vibrating middle 'C' fork near it. What will happen?"

"The first fork will vibrate; I remember the experiment from physics class in high school," he answered.

"What if I introduce a vibrating fork tuned to 'F'?"

"Nothing happens," he chimed in. "The two forks are vibrating at different frequencies, therefore are not in tune with each other. The first fork will register nothing."

"So, if there is no resonance—there is no energy exchange! Only when two fields are in tune or in harmony with each other is there an exchange of energy between them. When they enter each other's sphere, the stronger field transfers some of its energy to the weaker field, which is strengthened. This is the same law that governs the function of the mind," I added.

"What do you mean, governs the mind?" he quizzed.

"Let's demonstrate," I suggested.

"Don't think about the color of your car," I instructed. He looked a little puzzled. "What are you thinking about?"

"My blue car—resonance, I suppose?"

"Couldn't be anything else," I interjected.

"I could have decided to think about something else if I had wanted to," Richard shot back.

"Yes, but not without first deciding *not* to think about your car—which is thinking about your car," I said with a grin. "With my words I set up an energy field. Imagine your mind is like a filing cabinet and you have a file on 'cars.' My words resonated that file in your mind. In the same way that the tuning forks resonated and interchanged energy or information, your mind was stimulated into 'thought' about your car. **This action is not thinking at all, but simple resonance. It is the law that governs every process in the mind.** Words are a frequency put out by the human voice. **Our words resonate all information of similar frequencies in the mind that hears them. I call this the file folder effect.** Let me lay out that idea.

"All information that relates to any particular topic is stored in a 'file,' so to speak, with like information. When you fire one set of brain cells in the file, it sets up an energy field that tends to cause every other brain cell in that file to fire.

"In my workshops, I demonstrate the File Folder Effect by asking the audience to answer a question and shout their answers loudly enough to be heard. I then ask, 'What is the Lone Ranger's horse's name?' Throughout the audience I usually hear 'Silver,' the horse's name, 'Tonto' and 'Trigger.'

"I can see the audience responding in that way, michael, but I don't understand what that has to do with resonance."

"When I asked the horse's name each mind's file on 'old westerns' resonates as a result of the vibration set up by my voice. Every mind delivers its internal reality which is dependent not on my words, but on what my words resonate in each person in the audience. The same words are heard by every person but the reality triggered is totally dependent on what is stored in brain cells and which answer is closest to the surface in the resonated file. **The reality perceived always comes from the content of the listening mind, just like the meanings we give to life.**

"The *Law of Resonance* says that some of the energy of my voice transfers to the listener's brain cells containing realities about Silver. When the brain cells receive this energy, they fire and set up an internal vibration in that file. Every other brain cell in that file is then energized and tends to fire, hence Tonto and Trigger become possible answers, an expression of the File Folder Effect.

"If in our file on 'old westerns' Tonto or Trigger is closer to the surface than Silver, that becomes our answer, even though it is not directly related to the question. Some people actually call this automatic response mechanism 'thinking'! I suspect we would be amazed if we knew how many people's entire lives are governed by this process, governed and limited by the body's mind.

"The File Folder Effect is not thinking, it is only information firing in brain cells. It is information cycling in the body's mind in response to input—words, images, symbols, impulses or sensations.

Richard seemed intrigued with this concept and leaned toward me as he spoke. "Do you mean that anything that triggers brain cells can be a catalyst to the File Folder Effect?" he asked.

"Yes, and if we are run by that effect, we are run by the past. Recall that removing realities from a mind is called *Forgiveness* and is the key to taking charge of your life. **Developing the skill of managing the output of the mind makes one the operator of his or her own mind.**

"Richard, have you ever done anything you did not want to do?" I asked.

"Unfortunately, more often than I care to admit!"

"Why?"

There was a moment of hesitation before he spoke. "Fear, I guess. I didn't know any better, or maybe anger, a number of reasons, I suppose."

"The only reason we ever do *anything* is because we have a reality in our minds that guides us to do that particular form of behavior. A young boy, with limited realities in his mind, might smash a valued antique. Is the child destructive? No. He simply does not have the realties in his mind to guide him in what we consider the proper handling of something fragile."

Richard thought for a moment and made an insightful observation. "You mean, if he were told repeatedly, as a result of not knowing how to handle something, that he was bad and destructive, those words might build a reality into his mind? My God! That reality might actually drive him for his whole life?"

"If the child did not have access to the tool of *Forgiveness* and undo that reality, chances are he would be destructive for life, buying into the belief that he was born bad. Of course, there is no such thing as a bad child, but many 'bad children' are the product of parents and a culture who don't know any better nor understand their role in structuring the realities in a child's mind. The world would change overnight if the media comprehended and took responsibility for the realities they pump into children and the goals they present to innocent minds."

> ⚷ KEY THOUGHT—The mind is only capable of responding with whatever has been programmed into it. We can dismantle the realities that do not serve us by learning to *Forgive*.

He looked shocked. "This explains a lot of the violence and crime in our world. There is a saying that goes something like, 'It takes a whole community to raise a child.' It sounds to me like every interaction with the whole community has an influence in building each child's realities. That is an awesome responsibility.

"I used to think that parents who guarded carefully what their children did and with whom their children had contact were overprotective. Perhaps they understand the potential contribution the community makes in building their child's reality structure. This explains a lot about why children who have no contact with a healthy community, be it school or in a neighborhood, get into trouble. I'm going to do something about delivering what I have learned here today to children, schools, parents and teachers, michael." He sounded determined.

"We will be delighted to support your effort in any way we can, Richard. Many people who study this work become teachers of it. We invite anyone who feels it is their purpose to teach these tools to do so and to assist us in fulfilling our family's commitment of making these tools available to every mind on the planet. Let's look at the next phase in understanding the File Folder Effect.

"Words can be used to trigger files and realities, and 'hook' them together, so to speak. How long does it take to key realities together so they fire in concert with each other? Don't think about a *purple alligator*. Silly example, but if I see you in a week, a month, or year, and say 'Don't think about a purple _____,' what will your mind fill in the blank with?"

CONNECTING FILES TOGETHER IN A MIND

"Alligator, of course, but I probably won't even remember that a year from now," Richard chided.

"That may be true, but it illustrates the point. One of the things that puts an event into long-term memory is emotion. Repetition will drive the energy even deeper into the mind. Let's look at an all-too-typical example. Imagine, over the first decade or two of life, a young boy is taught, through being yelled at and punished, the conflicting thoughts that 'sex is dirty' and he should 'save it for the one he Loves.' Considering the File Folder Effect what results would you expect to see from those links in a mind?"

"Sounds like fertile ground for insanity," he blurted out.

"You got it! Until he can *Forgive* conflicting realities in his mind, anything that resonates sexuality will trigger: 'Sex is dirty, save it for the one you Love.' The resultant flow of realities will

     dr. michael ryce

probably leave him in confusion because hooked into those files, whenever they are resonated, are guilt, conflict and punishment. Do you see why negativity and punishment come into a marriage and violence results? Many people try to stay in control so they can live 'happily ever after,' which is another thought keyed to relationship. All this adds up to more and more confusion. Each of the main realities in these files is highly emotionally charged and linked together. What chance do you suppose that person has of a good marriage? What do you suppose the resulting reality flow will be in a spouse's mind, considering the File Folder Effect?"

"I suspect it will be pretty crazy, like I've been in my marriages," he replied grimly.

"Precisely! Confusion will be the result. Suppose we get two people in a marriage, each with similar realities, and they continuously resonate these kinds of brain cells in each other?"

"You mean like my marriages? Bedlam! It's insane! Divorce, pain, hatred and revenge. It's like being at war!" Richard wept in grief and rage. I sat quietly and held the space of Love as he processed through profound emotion.

> ⚷ KEY THOUGHT—The more we are able to presence Love for each other, the faster our healing proceeds.

I admired his courage in facing these buried issues. I thought about how so many of us have to be up against the wall before we are willing to confront ourselves. I suspect that is because we've been trained to numb our pain to the point where it takes a major crisis to break through our drugged state and get our attention. I reassured him it was safe to feel what was coming up and that facing these issues was how his healing would happen. Richard expressed his relief and confided that he had not felt emotions so deeply since he was a child. His face took on a radiance as some of the sorrow it had reflected earlier ebbed away.

We extended our example as we wondered what a couple living in a cabin in the woods would go through in adjusting to each other. Richard shared, "From my experience with intimate relationships, even that would be difficult."

I suggested we look at the same couple in the middle of New York City, dealing with each other and the complexities of their interactions. "Now compound all of that by adding the File Folder Effect which is exaggerated by all the stimulation of a metropolis.

"In the city, their senses are bombarded by movies, television, masses of people, magazines, newspapers, billboards, advertising in stores and on taxicabs and buses. These media continuously impale each spouse's mind with both subliminal and overt images of fear, guilt, sex, violence, hatred, drug and alcohol use and abuse. If their minds contain highly charged emotional realities connected to any of these issues, and they are continuously being resonated into activity, how sane can they be? Is it any wonder people turn to drugs and alcohol to cope?"

"This is overwhelming, michael! You are describing my life, and the life of almost everyone I know. I'm feeling like this is so big that we could never change it!" Richard said emphatically.

"That sounds like the world's brainwashing which says, 'You're powerless over what is happening. You're only one person, why don't you just give up and go along with the program.' I invite you to consider that the only part you need to do, Richard, is your own. You have as much power as *any* human being who has ever lived. You are capable of breaking through and making changes both within and without!

"The first step in convincing people change is impossible is to persuade them that pain is normal—it is not! **Due to the File Folder Effect, once pain is accepted in a mind, it can be hooked up to any reality in that mind through the use of words and images—and *any* image that pain hooks into, it distorts!** The more powerful the medium delivering the message, the greater is its potential for distorting the mind's output.

"Richard, just as you must look inside yourself if you want to heal, I'm suggesting we each must look at how we, as human beings, have created the insanities in our world. I know it starts to look overwhelming as we dig into these issues, but overwhelm is just a stage in the healing process.

"The issues we've been speaking of are at the root of the abuse we do and the abuse we experience in our relationships, our families, our communities, and our world. They are the source of the confusion that leads people to acts of violence, divorce, hatred, vengeance, crime and war. We must change these dynamics in ourselves if we are to thrive, which is what we are designed to do."

"You've lost me. I don't even know what you are talking about! How do you change dynamics that are so deeply ingrained?" he asked.

"*Forgiveness*! This tool of healing allows us to remove distorted realities from our minds. I'm talking about dealing with all the realities we have accepted that lead to confusion. So many people have bought into the 'Sex is dirty, save it for the one you Love' and other insane lines of thinking, that relationship and family seem doomed in our culture. *True Forgiveness* of all painful realities is where our healing lies. If we refuse to do our healing work, we can be easily manipulated and controlled by anyone who knows how to push our buttons.

"I'm referring to having the basic skill of removing realities that do not serve us, and at the risk of sounding patronizing, Richard, the overwhelmed feeling you have is exactly my point. We've resonated all those realities inside of you during our conversation today. Notice it is a beautiful autumn day and we are safe and secure on our deck in the Ozarks. We even have clean air to breathe. The only difference between the beginning of our conversation and now is the realities that have been resonated in your mind. Notice, nothing has changed in the world. The only thing different is what has been stirred up in your mind. You are in overwhelm only because of that. This is the beginning of some deep processing which will probably continue for months to come. A little overwhelm is to be expected."

"Okay, I can accept that, but I don't understand what is happening. Why all the confusion?" he asked.

"Richard, the nature of thoughts is energy and they follow the laws of energy. I suspect they have both wave and particle properties, much like light. If I shine a red, a blue and a green light on a plain white surface, what will you see?"

"I'll see a red, green and blue light reflecting off the surface if you shine them one at a time, or, if you shine them all on one spot, there will be a mixing of the colors," he answered with raised eyebrows and a puzzled look.

"Bear with me, there is a point to this," I offered. "When realities are resonated in a mind, their properties are much like the light. If they surface, one at a time, like the single light shining on a spot, there will be clarity in the thoughts behind that reality and confusion will be impossible. However, if several conflicting realities try to surface simultaneously, like the three lights shining on one spot, there will be a mix—a confusion in the thoughts that generate the conflicting realities.

"Richard, I've become aware of a few issues for myself to work out and heal from today's conversation. I'm sure we have fired some realities for you to deal with in our interaction. Until you remove the conflicts, and clarify your reality structure for yourself, confusion will tend to be the result of such a process."

"Well, the File Folder Effect is taking its toll on me at this moment. If a conversation such as the one we are having stirs up this much feeling, what chance does the average person have in life?" Richard asked.

"Most people don't allow the space in their lives to look this deeply into themselves. They keep themselves drugged and on the run with no time to feel their feelings. If hidden feelings surface during dinner, another scotch or serving of a sugar-laden dessert will take care of keeping those feelings suppressed. If the drugs from the night before slow their waking process in the morning, people often jump start themselves with caffeine, nicotine and/or sugar. This behavior is so prevalent it is not recognized for what it is—addiction and suppression. Busy-ness is another of the drugs used in our culture to avoid looking at our issues.

"Layers of confusion will surface as you do your work and that is desirable. As conflicting realities surface and you forgive them, new levels of clarity and empowerment will come. This will happen if you do not use your energy or drugs to avoid, numb out and stuff what you don't want to see. Healing will occur, instead, if you deal with and release the painful realities and let go of the burdens that most people suppress and keep hidden."

"You resonate hope in me, michael. It looks like a giant task, but the other way of living hasn't worked, so why not do it differently?" Richard's energy seemed to lighten a little and I asked him why. "Well, even though I've dug myself into a pit, I think I'm starting to see a way out. I'm grasping the cause and the solution to the insanity that I have experienced all my life. I'm seeing a light at the end of the tunnel, and this time it's not an oncoming train. I think I can actually get a handle on what has happened," he said enthusiastically. "I might even be able to create a decent, Loving relationship with this understanding and these tools."

> ☞ KEY THOUGHT—We must reach the point where we can change our present in order to change our future.

"The goal of this work is to empower people to become conscious of everything in their lives. **People who are not conscious operators of their own minds can be programmed by others to react with *any* reality in response to *any* situation.**

"When it comes to deciding whether or not to do your work, Richard, what else is there to do? Once you see that your whole life flows from your inner dynamics, how else can you proceed but to commit yourself and move forward?"

"I could see myself just sinking into oblivion, becoming a hermit in Wyoming. I could just quit!"

"True, but that would say to me that you didn't really hear or develop enough brain cells to see that there is something you can do about your life and about the world. It is not unusual for me to hear from people who attended one of my workshops ten or fifteen years ago. They often tell me they thought I was nuts back then, but a phrase or an idea stuck with them. Then they saw examples of that idea often enough that things finally clicked. They decided they had to know more about the principles of this work.

"It's like the parable of the sowing of the seeds. Even if one does not do his or her 'mind gardening,' sooner or later these ideas take hold sufficiently to form sensible realities in a mind. This work is innate knowledge for people. I'm not teaching them anything they don't already know. It's just a matter of the inner Truth breaking through the layers of insane realities that have been accepted in the mind. Once you clear up the twisted ideas and clean out the corrupted files, this work becomes natural.

"This information should be kindergarten stuff, conversations children have on the playground, yet it is all but missing from our culture," I said. "The absence of an understanding of Love is the reason it is so rare, I suspect."

"Let's look at some of the questions you asked earlier about Love, Richard."

dr. michael ryce

18

CLARIFYING LOVE

Richard and I went back to our discussion of Love. I put forward the thought that one of the keys to this process is clarifying the idea of Love, which has been ill-defined, misused and distorted. Cleaning up its definition in our minds is an important piece of foundational work.

Two thousand years ago, we were taught Love was the most important Law to human existence—it must come first if intelligence is to be maintained. Teaching Love is not religious, it is the most practical thing in the world. One of the major pitfalls we humans have fallen into is that of making any teaching on Love sound like religion. Many people throw out teachings based on Love, or only give them lip service because they think those teachings are religion, which they have been subtly taught to reject.

Richard thought that the ideas on Love sounded good, but wanted to know how to Love someone who had just been abusive to him. He said in an exasperated tone, "Who could feel anything but anger and hate in that situation?"

"To Love, you must first straighten out your definition of the word. This may sound trite, Richard, but the people who can feel Love when attacked know what Love is and do not have realities called anger and hate in them."

"But . . ." Richard interjected.

"Stay with me for a minute. Remember, our goal is to let go of the old beliefs and manipulative teachings long enough to build some new brain cells. If, when I am finished, what I have said does not make sense, throw it out and go back to the old way.

"Love, in Aramaic, does not mean cooperate with and help the person who is beating up on you. It does not mean accept every atrocity with a smile and pretend that all is well when it is not. Love does not mean that you don't hold people accountable for their behavior. Love is not a passive state of suppressing your anger so you look like a saint," I reported.

"So, it's okay to get angry when someone abuses you!" Richard said gleefully. "I thought so!"

"The reality in your head is giving you information that was not delivered by my words, Richard. It's okay to get angry with someone if you want your mind to be stupid while you interact with them," I replied.

> ⚬━┳ KEY THOUGHT—A mind without Love is "stupid."

"What is that supposed to mean?" Richard almost shouted. "It sounds like you're playing games with me and I don't like it!"

"There is an old saying that the Truth will set you free, but first it's going to make you very, very angry," I said half-jokingly, in an attempt to lighten the energy a little.

"Richard, the word Love in this culture is so distorted that its true meaning is almost lost. Much of the entertainment industry would have us believe Love is sexual athletics and satiation. Others would have us believe it is self-denial and sacrifice. Still others would have us think we show Love by receiving their abuses graciously. Think about it. Who has something to gain by our believing in these bizarre definitions of Love?" I could almost hear Richard's brain churning in search of an answer.

"I'm not sure what you mean."

"If I believe Love is sexual athletics as portrayed on the screen," I suggested, "might I pay for more sick movies and demand more intense and bizarre sexuality in order to be satiated? Might I think what is played out in movies is normal and try to live up to the reality I've come to believe is true? Might I find myself wanting to participate in the outrageous habits for which much of the entertainment industry is famous?

"We need to recognize, Richard, that fulfilling outrageous fantasies will never satisfy us, it will only lead to even more bizarre behaviors. Until we do, we will continue to repeat those behaviors, wondering, 'Is that all there is? What's wrong with me?' If we hold painful realities in our minds, it does not matter how many of the 'rewards' based on an incorrect understanding of life we receive, happiness will still elude us. No matter how many possessions, how much money, sex, power or fame we achieve, these things can never satisfy us because they are empty and false. **Satiation masquerades as satisfaction, but when it is experienced, it cannot deliver its tempting guarantee.**"

> ⚷ KEY THOUGHT—Possessions can not take the place of happiness.

I told Richard that I had always enjoyed the story of the old man on his deathbed who was asked for the secret to happiness. The old man is said to have replied, "For years and years I searched for what people told me would make me happy, and then I decided to be happy without it." **Happiness is a state of mind, a choice we make, not a result of possessing things or being in control of people or circumstances. People often use the sensation that comes from possessing things as a**

substitute for happiness, for relationship and as a way of not dealing with their internalized pain.

"Real relationship is dead in the glamour industry's definition of Love. Have you ever felt used as a sexual object and then thrown away? Anyone who buys into the common media definition of Love becomes a sexual object in their own mind and in the minds of others. Of course, like other objects, they are thrown away after use," I added.

"I've been on both sides of that scenario," Richard said sadly, "and I don't understand why it has to be that way. I would Love to be in a true, honest and real relationship. Perhaps that is impossible until I straighten out some of my conflicting realities."

"I think you are right. We tend to live exactly what we have learned, and if we have been used and abused, it takes work to live differently. Relationships are a wondrous place for nurturing, support and healing if we can remove the confusing and conflicting realities we have hooked into them. My experience of people who reject or cannot form long-term relationships is they have so much pain in their 'relationship file,' they have to keep on the move or they will have to face what is hidden inside of them."

"I've been on the run too long," Richard chimed in. "Who promotes this insanity, why is there so much confusion in the world?" he asked.

"To answer that, notice who receives the benefits of a twisted understanding of Love. Anyone who distorts Truth to gain something for themselves is in so much pain and lives in such inward poverty that they cannot live honestly. They think they must manipulate to have anything for themselves—to survive.

"Have you ever noticed that the promoter of the idea that 'Love is self-sacrifice' always has their hand out, and those who feed on abusing others push the idea that Love is the gracious acceptance of their abuse? Those who promote Love as sex have a lot more sex objects of whom to take advantage, and those with a victim mentality get the benefit of playing out the role to which they are dedicated," I added.

"I'm not quite keeping up with everything you're saying, but I get its importance. I suppose I have to clean up some of the clouds I've allowed my mind to accept and build more brain cells about what Love really is before I will fully grasp it. However, you've got my attention again. I have a question that has bothered me all my life, michael. What is Love?"

"I don't know what it is," came my unexpected reply.

"What? Why are we having this discussion about Love if you can't even tell me what it is?" he demanded.

"I didn't say I don't have any ideas, Richard. I just hesitate to reduce such an important matter to words. Words are too small for such a topic. In Aramaic, it appears that Love is what we are, it is the 'stuff' of human existence. Without it, we are not human, but reduced to less than animal status. In the Aramaic Scriptures, we are told that we are made in the image and likeness of the Creator and that the Creator is Love.

> ○━┳ KEY THOUGHT—If the offspring of an elephant is an elephant and the offspring of a dog is a dog, what is the offspring of Love?

"Do you remember, when you were a child, looking around at the way the world worked and knowing in your heart it was supposed to be about something other than what you were seeing, something other than the almost universal strife?

"Look into the eyes of a child. How many times, on an energy level, must that child be violated to cause him to hate? How much propaganda does it take to grow a child into a person who can kill, into a person who believes that the world is a fearsome place—that life is poverty, relationships hell and sex dirty? What does it take for people to believe they are sinners, condemned by a Creator called Love in Whose Image they are made? Why is there such confusion in the world? For the answer, check out who benefits from programmed unconsciousness."

"I'm not sure if this is what you mean," Richard interjected, "but I can think back to being a kid, watching the hypocrites fight and belittle each other, and I knew that was not how we were supposed to behave. I kept coming back to my abusers with trust and total Love, and kept getting wiped out," Richard said sadly.

"So you took on their behavior?" I asked.

"What?! I wouldn't do that!" he protested.

"Are you sure?" I queried.

"I've never been abusive, I've never hit anybody in my life!"

"Have you ever withdrawn Love, put down or tried to control others for your own benefit? Have you used anger, money or things to manipulate others into behaving the way you wanted?" I inquired. "Have you ever withheld Love from yourself?"

"Well, yes, but that's not abuse," he said, looking defensive.

"Think back to being the kid that kept Loving those that abused him—he only wanted one thing—to be Loved. How did he feel when Love was withheld and he was manipulated with money, threats and put-downs?" I asked quietly, aware that some very tender feelings were surfacing in him.

"Abused," he replied quietly. I sensed tears just under the surface, tears that had been held inside for a long time.

"It feels to me like there might be a lot of sadness, grief and uncried tears wanting to let loose, Richard."

"I was taught it was wrong to cry," his voice cracked as he tried to hide his sadness.

dr. michael ryce

"That is another reality with which we've been brainwashed. Macho doesn't work. **If we cannot accurately feel our feelings, we are out of touch with an important guidance system.** Recall, Richard, the operative principle here is **'If I'm in pain, I'm in error.'** The pain is an attempt on the part of the *body* to warn you of error and be of help.

"Notice, you felt abused when all the things you normally do to people, yourself included, were done to you as a child," I pointed out.

"You mean I am an abuser? I've never thought of myself that way. I always considered myself a nice guy. I thought what I was doing was normal," he added.

"These are behaviors that few have escaped. It is an almost universal phenomenon, an opportunity for healing that virtually every one of us gets. Unfortunately, abuse and exploitation have become 'normal' for many people, but that does not make it 'natural.' Remember when, as a child, you knew life was about Love and abuse was a foreign concept? I believe that abuse can be inherited, but usually it must be learned.

"People stuck in the mind-set of the world—whether teacher, parent, politician or minister—through the denial of Loving feelings and the use of abuse, help to build many distorted realities into peoples' minds. The distorted realities are then used to control and exploit. This is done with our cooperation, and the realities we choose to identify with direct us to live in a way other than our natural inclination, which is to Love."

☞ KEY THOUGHT—"All exploitation is based on co-operation, willing or forced, of the exploited. However much we may detest admitting it, the fact remains that there would be no exploitation if people refused to obey the exploiter."

Mahatma Gandhi. *India of My Dreams*

"I can kind of remember when I knew I shouldn't treat people the way I do." Richard almost sounded like a child as he spoke. "I always wanted to be Loving to people, but was hurt so often I guess I hardened myself to the effects of my abrasive behaviors and my tendency to bully people."

We explored the idea of abuse and came to the conclusion that **abuse and withholding Love are learned responses.** It became apparent from our discussion that the reality structure in most people's minds, which is formed as a result of their distorted learning experiences, determines their behavior. Each distorted experience is a result of the combination of internal realities interacting with environmental influences.

"In Aramaic, blocking awareness of abusive behaviors, of Love and/or of feelings was called 'hardening the heart,'" I explained. "Each hardened heart is convinced that to act in accord with its distorted reality structure is 'normal.' When we can't feel, we can be convinced to do all sorts of insane things to ourselves and others and think it's normal." We observed, each from our own experience, that a person with a hardened heart remains convinced his actions are right when *he does* them, even though he says *others* are insane when *they do* exactly the same things.

Richard reiterated his understanding of what he called "that intriguing attribute" of the mind: **Blockage of Truth. "A mind in denial literally hides information from itself; it does not see information contrary to what it believes."**

"That seems to be how it works," I affirmed. "If we hold an emotionally charged goal of being right, the mind hides all evidence that enables us to see the Truth. The only thing available is error. Think about people who abuse but deny it. They reinterpret their behavior to justify it or blot the Truth out of awareness so they can continue to think of themselves as 'right.' The Truth of the abuse they do is invisible to them. This is a condition that can be corrected only by the Love of Truth.

"Have you ever, for little or no apparent reason, been abruptly thrown out of someone's life or, perhaps, thrown someone out and wondered why?"

"As a matter of fact, I was just thinking about a time when a seemingly close friendship ended over an inconsequential argument," Richard answered. "She blamed me for something I knew nothing about, and there was no way to convince her to think about it differently. I've often wondered why that happened, but I think you just explained it. I am understanding it for the first time. Her mind could only give her the evidence she needed to make me wrong rather than accept responsibility. Blocking my input was her way to protect herself. Her 'heart was hardened against the Truth.'" Richard seemed deep in thought as he spoke.

"If you want to do an interesting experiment, show someone evidence of a Truth they do not want to see. Unless they Love Truth deeply, they will:

1. Tell you that you are crazy or imagining things, or they 'forget' the event ever happened.

2. Leave, physically, by making an excuse or, mentally, by wandering off to other topics and not acknowledging the conversation you are attempting to have with them.

3. Turn on you with some form of manipulation, usually anger, to stop you from presenting your information or accuse you of a similar defect, telling you about a time when you did the same thing as though that justifies their behavior and 'makes them right.'

4. Attack you fiercely, in a manner that is all out of proportion to the issue involved. You will wonder what hit you. Chances are you will end up unwelcome in that person's life.

"If you continue to present the evidence they are in denial about, be prepared to duck so you keep your head," I said, half-jokingly, "because there is so much insanity in our culture."

"I recognize that experiment and have been attacked for doing exactly what you describe, but do you really believe that many people are crazy?" he questioned.

"I am talking about insanity, not craziness, Richard. **In this work, an 'insane mind' is defined as one that lacks the condition of Love. A mind without Love is a mind without real choices, therefore 'insane.'**

"In Aramaic thought, it was known that without Love, humans were easy to take advantage of, weak and vulnerable. Love is a major key because it inoculates the mind against insane behavior," I offered. "That is why it was called the *First Law*. A lack of awareness of this *Law* is the recipe for insanity."

He broke in, "I'm lost again. This starts to make sense, and then the sensible part seems to evade me."

"That's what happens when building brain cells. **The realities that show up in your mind from newly developed brain cells are fragile and easily distorted by conflicting realities from the past.** That is why I ask people to investigate, think on these ideas for themselves and not believe a word I am saying."

"Oh, come on, michael. Obviously, you're saying all of what you do, so people believe it," he said, with a touch of sarcasm.

"Actually, Richard, no. I say what I say to build a different framework and tools with which to experience life differently. A thought system built on someone else's experience is just a belief system and will tend to crumble under pressure.

"For instance, you asked earlier about a definition for Love. I don't have one, but I do know a way to experience it and what signals tell you when Love is present."

"What are the signals that tell you Love is present?" he asked.

"First, the mind that holds the condition of Love—in the ancient Aramaic 'Perfect Love'—is peaceful and patient *in all circumstances*. This mind takes responsibility for any disturbance it has and, therefore, heals itself quickly and creates a space of healing for others. Additional fruit the mind of Love includes is *tenderness, compassion* and *gentleness*.

"A mind that proclaims it punishes and brandishes fear in the name of Love is either *deceiving* or is a *deceived* mind. No such fruit is *possible* from Love."

"That makes sense out of a lot of senselessness I've seen," Richard sighed. "What did you mean when you said you had a way to experience Love?"

"We could call this an experiential definition: Love is what you experience just after you use *True Forgiveness*. It is what is left when the mind's realities get out of the way. Now, if I tell you that and you believe it, we will have another belief system in the world, another belief system to fight over and defend.

"If you use the tools and have a personal experience, *personally experienced*, is there anything to fight over? No. Only the insecure who don't know what Love is, have to force and fight over their B.S.—their *Belief Systems*. Only the insecure need to have everyone believe the same way they do so that their beliefs will not be challenged.

> ⚷ Key Thought—An experiential definition of Love: What you experience just after *True Forgiveness*.

"Richard, each of us was created in a state of Love and we deserve to experience that state twenty four hours a day, seven days a week. If we are not experiencing it, something is out of place. When we withhold Love from another, it is we who suffer from the withdrawl of that Love, it is we who experience the lack of Love. *Re-member* what you knew as a child about the way the world was supposed to operate?

"My function in the world is to deliver tools to people and point them toward the results possible with the use of the tools. My goal is to inspire you to use the tools and then arrive at your own conclusions about life. Of course, I think when the evidence is in, this work will prove itself correct, but the world does not need another belief system. It needs the *experience* of Love.

"Love, in Aramaic, is a condition in the mind that each individual is responsible for maintaining. It is the fuel that empowers the human mind to function correctly.

"Without Love, the mind is dysfunctional and we do insane things. Tell me, Richard, when are you most intelligent? When do you have the most flexibility, the widest range of choices and the highest levels of creativity? Is it when you are angry? Afraid? Hostile?" I asked.

"Obviously, most everything I've ever done and regretted was done when I was in one of those states. Let me be clear on this. Are you saying that Love is the key to intelligence?" he inquired.

"If intelligence means the ability to choose, yes. Notice when a choice is made in anger or upset—a lack of Love—it is no choice at all. We are simply driven by resonance—emotional realities from our past—driven to do things, often against our own will and choice. *This only happens in a mind that lacks Love*," I emphasized.

"This lack of Love, which compromises intelligence, has led most of humanity to be shackled to religious and political systems based on fear. We need to understand how to forgive our fears, or as said in the Aramaic Scriptures, 'cast out' the 'demon' fear. If we do not we will find ourselves unwittingly acting in support of that demon. A mind without the condition of Love promotes and reinforces fear at every turn. No true Spiritual teacher who understands how life and the mind operate uses fear to motivate."

> ☞ KEY THOUGHT—"The greatest help you can give me is to banish fear from your hearts." Mahatma Gandhi, *Ramanama*

Richard broke in. "I have seen fear motivate people to do the right things."

"In the short term, I agree. You can get people to do things out of fear. Have you noticed the long term result is always a disaster? For instance, a parent forces a child with threats and abuse. The child obeys the parent out of fear; but, in the end, hates them and passes the force and abuse on to others. The reason is **the tools used to produce a result will always produce a result like the tools. Children are 'learning sponges;' they are believing creatures. What they live with, they learn, and then they live whatever it is they have learned.**"

"This makes too much sense!" Richard's whole being seemed to confirm his agreement with my words.

"Yes, and **there is a peace when one achieves a practical understanding of tools that work and has the intellectual basis to reinforce that understanding.** This work draws on all disciplines in order to build a solid foundation for the undoing of unconsciousness and for a life that is harmonious and peaceful. With its synthesis of different disciplines, it is a big chunk to bite off and chew.

"It takes patience and time to build the brain cells and integrate each of the disciplines upon which this work is built. That foundation is what makes these tools fully available. Some unconsciousness as you undo the patterns of the past and move into understanding and knowledge is to be expected. Allowing deeper issues to surface, in the presence of Love, burns them off, so to speak. If you are willing to look into yourself, your family interactions and the dynamics of the culture, healing accelerates.

"An unwillingness to look deeper means that old patterns will tend to be passed on and played out by the next generation. Conscious, Active, Present Love is the key to healing whatever needs to be healed."

"What is the best tool for really, truly getting to the space of Love within relationships with children, spouses or myself, and healing those generational patterns?" Richard inquired.

"When someone triggers a healing opportunity, the first thing to do is choose to be responsible for your mind's output, forgive and learn to hold the condition of Love in your mind in all circumstances—*regardless of what your mind prompts you to do*. We call that kind of Love all-encompassing Love. The tool, *My Commitment*, from the *Healing Through Relationships* workshop was developed to assist in creating that space of Love. It is a powerful key to staying on track and keeping Love in your mind when you feel turmoil. It is the best reminder I have found to get me back to a Loving space when upset surfaces. Speak it at least daily in your closest relationships and say it aloud to yourself while looking in the mirror."

My Commitment

♡ I promise to TRUST you enough
to tell you the Truth and treat you
LOVINGLY, Gently and with Respect.
I will do this in my thoughts, words and actions,
whether in your presence or not.

♡ In every interaction I will look for and
acknowledge the Highest and Best in you
as I surrender to LOVE, our true nature.
My connection to my Source and nurturing
my relationship with you is always
more important than any issue.

♡ If anything unlike LOVE comes up, I will hold
us in my heart and listen as I learn to speak,
experience and be RESPONSIBLE
for my own realities. I am here for and with you.
I will keep communication open and keep
LOVE Conscious, Active and Present
as we HEAL and CELEBRATE LIFE!

michael & marijo

Notes

dr. michael ryce

19

INHERITED PATTERNS

As Richard and I reviewed some of his family dynamics, we processed several issues he had with his mother. I suggested that it might be valuable to consider that his mother probably came by her behavior, her "off the mark" patterns, the same way he did. He acknowledged that she very likely never saw what she did as abuse, but rather as a way to protect herself, as he had.

"Abuse," I said, "is one behavior that tends to be transmitted from generation to generation. Facing and processing through the abusive patterns is the best way I know to stop the behavior from being passed on to our children. This work is about taking on the generations, for the generations. **What you don't deal with will be passed on; what you are willing to face, sort out and heal will no longer infect family dynamics. The pattern then stops with you!**"

"Does that mean my daughter has the same issues as I do? You mean if I heal, she won't have to deal with them?"

"It is very probable that she grew up reacting in some way to the same issues as you do. I'd be willing to bet that you have unintentionally treated her in a similar fashion to the way your mother treated you.

THE CHAIN OF ABUSE

"As you heal the issues with your mother, not only will your relationship with her improve, most likely your relationship with your daughter will shift as well," I assured him.

"Sometimes my daughter avoids me like the plague, and I've always wondered why. Now I think I know. She used to tell me I treated her poorly, but I never listened. I didn't see it that way. I guess my mom didn't either. Come to think of it, my mom used to brush me off the same way my daughter says I do to her. It feels like a relief to know that I can do things differently and develop a more Loving relationship with her. You know, I'm feeling pretty good. I think I might be feeling that 'empowerment' feeling you were talking about earlier. For the first time in a long time, I'm feeling like I can do something about my life."

dr. michael ryce

"Richard, my mind keeps going back to a thought I had when we were talking about your issues around your mother. Would you be willing to look at that?"

He spoke with hesitation. "What the heck, I feel pretty good, considering what I've been through today. If someone told me I could uncover and deal with events and issues of such proportions as I have and come out the other side with a smile on my face, I'd have said they were crazy."

"Recall that the key to process and healing is holding the space of Love. Bringing these issues to the surface in another setting could lead to craziness," I acknowledged.

"Is this the kind of thing that people do at your intensive workshops?" he asked.

"That is the focus. In an intensive, we work to give the best tools and understanding possible. The rest is process, and it is like watching miracles happen when a number of people get together to do healing work," I replied.

"I know you wouldn't engage me in this conversation to avoid looking at the issue I asked about," I said with a chuckle. "Are you willing to look at that one?"

"I'm willing," he said as a trace of fear flashed across his face.

"Have you ever thought that living with you might be like walking through a minefield?" I inquired.

"No, of course not!" came his indignant reply.

"Are you feeling defensive, Richard?"

"Perhaps a little, wouldn't you be?"

"Probably. I want to be clear that the purpose of bringing things to the surface is to gently look, own them and let go of what does not work. I'm on your team and want to support you in that process. Has anyone ever given you that feedback about a minefield before?"

Richard did admit that he had been told, more than once, that living with him was like walking on eggshells. He again affirmed that he had never thought of himself in that way.

"Seldom do we see ourselves as others see us, and most people never take the time to *listen* to what others are *really* saying. **Truly taking the time to listen to others provides us with the opportunity to look differently at unconsciously driven behavior, as does being aware of our responses to what others say.**"

> ⚷ KEY THOUGHT—Your relationships and your words are mirrors of your mind.

I spoke about his making a practice of searching for his patterns of unconscious, driven behavior. I reminded him of our opening conversation—or mis-conversation—about responsibility. "Recall, Richard, we each experienced the same actuality, we each *heard* identical words, but your *listening* spoke to you of fault and blame, while mine informed me of 'response-ability.' Remember the upset that surfaced for you and how much hostility you expressed?"

"Actually, I didn't express nearly as much as I felt at the moment!" he informed me.

"When upset surfaces, we call it an opportunity to learn to *Forgive*—an opportunity to learn to let go of the tendency to blame others for what they trigger in us.

"Most people tend to experience their mind's interpretation of an event in the world and think that is what is actually happening. We tend to think ours is the only Truth. Like ripples distort an image on the surface of a pond, there is always some distortion of the images output from the mind when we are in upset. The Truth cannot be reflected accurately in a disturbed mind."

132

"If I'm clear on the bottom line of this work it is that at *every* moment we are each experiencing our own reality, correct? You're saying that our realities are made up of internal information *and not caused by outside events?* What we have been trained to think of as an actual event in the world is really happening in our heads, and what happens in our heads is distorted by upsets and grievances we hold?" Richard looked at me for confirmation.

"The world repeatedly triggers the realities we hold onto and then we wonder, '*Why Is This Happening To Me . . . AGAIN?!*' Recall now that projection is blaming our inner happenings on others. When in blame, the tendency is to think the outside event is causing your experience. *It is not!*

"Projection does not work to alleviate pain because when you pretend the problem is outside, you leave the pain inside and cut yourself off from being able to resolve it. The reason running away does not work to put an end to your pain is that you take your painful realities with you. Has moving ever done much to change the quality of your relationships?"

"No. I guess avoidance is not the answer."

We talked about the idea that anger does not work and is never justified. We also explored the stresses involved in holding anger in the *body* and the pain from the tensions of keeping falsehoods in place. We considered the possibility that as these patterns are passed on, they might contribute to what is now thought of as genetically inherited dis-ease. "Is it possible that family dis-ease patterns can be changed, michael?" Richard asked.

"Absolutely! My experience is that **holding the space of Conscious, Active, Present Love while unresolved issues surface can shift any energy pattern.**"

Richard was reaching new levels of clarity and enthusiasm in his process. Anyone who has done this work knows that the event that follows a new level of empowerment is a Healing Crisis. It is at this point in the process that many people become filled with self-doubt about their ability to truly heal their pain. For some, the process seems too hard, too complicated; for some, too simple; and for others, the pain seems too deep. He looked forlorn as old feelings of hopelessness surfaced for healing.

"This sounds so hopeless! If all of my pain is inside of me, how can I ever hope to get away from it? Why are we not all taught as children that we create our own reality? How will I ever work this out in my relationships? How can I ever... ?"

"Slow down, Richard. Remember, these feelings will pass! The surfacing of hopelessness is an opportunity to deal with that reality in your mind. You are at least learning these things now! Most people go through their entire lives without ever discovering what is going on, without *ever* having tools.

> ○━┳ KEY THOUGHT—Upset is an opportunity to learn *Forgiveness* and to let go of blame.

"As for your question about why we were not taught this as children, Benjamin Franklin made a statement that sums it up perfectly: *'You will observe with concern how long a useful Truth may be known and exist, before it is generally received and practiced upon.'*

"Richard, I have some good news and some bad news. The reason for your distress is your new level of empowerment. Your pain signals the opportunity to be aware of patterns that do not work, and heal them. That's the good news."

"Shouldn't my new level of empowerment make me feel better, michael?"

"Definitely, but first the blocks to that empowerment being actualized in your life must be surfaced and healed. Everything unlike your empowerment must be *Forgiven*. This is only possible when you have reached a higher level of vitality than your norm."

20

HEALING CRISES

"Richard, the bad news is: Rather than run away from pain, we need to face it, escape is not a part of the process. Reaching new levels of empowerment, as you have, also gives you the strength to delve into new depths of your healing, which is not always Dr. Feelgood. As you recognize the next level of your work it is important to remember the Cosmic Grease—willingness.

"Moving into the release mode, as you have, old energies from the past are felt as though they are present moment experiences—they are not! Things seem the darkest because you are accessing new depths, hidden perhaps for years, maybe even for generations. This part of your work is called a Healing Crisis.

"Healing Crises are usually experienced on three levels. When an energy goes into the human system, it creates symptoms. When the symptoms of a degenerative energy are suppressed, as with the use of drugs, they do not leave the system but are driven deep into tissue. This happens whether the suppressed energy is physical, mental or emotional. Symptomatically, each release of old dis-ease energies is experienced and felt in the same way, with the same intensity, as when they entered the system as disease. Willingness is the Cosmic Grease that accelerates and eases the process of release.

"On a physical level, as the energy releases, it looks like old physical symptoms and low energy. On the mental level, release looks like any kind of negative thought, and on the emotional level it feels like any old feeling that has ever been suppressed. Release can also put in its appearance as depression. These are all desirable states, Richard."

"R-i-g-h-t, michael. In the past, I would have accused you of being crazy, but I'm really starting to hear you with different ears. It's a strange sensation finding myself saying I'm willing to purposely experience pain. I have one problem, though. If I'm going to experience all these symptoms, how will I know if I'm in one of these Healing Crises or if I'm sick?"

"Ultimately, you must be in touch with what is going on in your system and make the determination for yourself as to the nature of your symptoms. There are three signals which can assist you in determining whether or not symptoms are healing in process. They are:

☑ First, you've reached a new level of vitality.

☑ Second, you are doing your inner work and more and more of the 'right' things.

☑ Third, there is an increase in elimination. Any or all of the eliminative channels—the skin, lungs, bowel, bladder or mucus membranes—increase their output.

"If your answer to all three of these signals is 'yes' when you are symptomatic, you are likely in a Healing Crisis. It's time to use the tools, rest, and remember the Cosmic Grease—Be Willing!"

> ⊶ᴛ KEY THOUGHT—When in pain, you have two choices. One is healing. Any other choice, no matter what it is, leaves you in your pain.

21

WAKING FROM THE HAS BIN

"In each Healing Crisis, you will have the opportunity to question different realities fed to you by your mind. It is a chance to review and make decisions based on principles, rather than having to accept and be directed by whatever happens to be triggered in you. The reason for doing this, even though it *appears* you are experiencing the present moment through your mind, is that *all* experience from the human mind is from the past. **The present moment cannot be experienced through the mind.**"

"I can't even relate to that thought, michael. How else can I experience life but through my mind? Obviously, what comes from the mind is from the present." Richard appeared to be in resistance to a new idea again.

"Recall the analogy of the two-dimensional creature? She assured us that a basketball was a series of flat planes experienced over time, right? How did we finally get her to see the basketball as it is? She had to *question everything*, including her own experience. It was not until she did, that the possibility of a new experience opened for her. It is amazing how many people want change but *refuse* to think or act differently."

I explained to Richard an experiment I do in my workshops. I ask everyone in the audience to step back from their minds and observe what happens inside. I then ask them to put their right hand on their right ear and invite everyone to look around and notice that each person is doing pretty much the same thing.

> ☞ KEY THOUGHT—Another key to healing: Give yourself permission to experience life differently.

"Why did they all do the same action and put their right hand to their right ear, Richard?"

"They followed your directions."

"I have another theory. In each mind there are brain cells storing information from the past. Each person was trained in what the words 'right,' 'hand' and 'ear' meant. When I spoke, I caused those brain cells to fire, and each was shown the reality contained in their brain cell structure and followed the directions given to them by that reality. They did not follow my directions."

"Of course, they followed your directions!" he protested.

"The instructions, *'Put your right hand on your ear,'* came from my voice, true. The *reality* each mind had for those words came from the past of each individual involved in the exercise. The only reason each person did the same thing is that they were all taught the same realities about *'right,' 'hand'* and *'ear.'* They didn't follow my directions, but the directions that came from their minds, from the past."

"Interesting theory, michael, but how do we verify it?"

"I thought you might ask that, Richard. Imagine that we have somebody in the audience whose mother trained him differently. Imagine his mother taught him that the *nose* is an ear. Where did he put his hand when I said 'Put your right hand on your right ear?'"

138   dr. michael ryce

"He would put his hand to his nose, of course."

"Put that in the context of our search to verify that everything from the mind is from the past. I gave one set of instructions but two different results were produced. One person was out of step with everyone else and put his hand on his nose, which he had been taught was an ear. Was anyone following my instructions? I offer that each person followed the guidance of the reality that my instruction *triggered* in them, and that guidance came from the past in each mind, not from my words.

"Had I spoken my instructions in Chinese, would anyone have moved a hand? Only those who spoke Chinese. Otherwise nothing from the past was triggered in anyone's mind by the words I spoke.

"Richard, put your right hand on your gizzard."

He paused a moment, "I can't do that, I don't have one!"

"Notice, though you have no gizzard, you still looked through your past, in your Has Bin, your mind, to check and see if there was a reality there that could give meaning to my words. No information in brain cells? No past from which to gather a meaning! With no past, there was no reality to project onto my words.

"Whether your mind gives its meaning in an instant, as when I said 'Put your right hand on your right ear,' or whether there is a time delay as in looking for your gizzard, every meaning from the mind is from the past. Each meaning is an individual reality projected onto my words.

"The mind's meanings are all from the past. The mind, known as the 'great deceiver,' subtly deceives us into thinking its information is the Truth and what is happening now, *in the present*. All 'thought' is from the past.

"If all of the information in our brain cell structure has come from the external world, our reality structures have been totally molded by that world. When we unconsciously lend our creative power to our past, we can become lost in recreating it—the essence of the *Why Is This Happening To Me . . . AGAIN?!* experience. When we awaken from the sleep induced by existing in the shadow of a dead past and a dead mind, we find that Love, Aliveness, Joy and Delight are our birthright and anything less is a lie. If you doubt that, just look into the eyes of a child. The only reason we live in anything less than our birthright is that we are living out of the content of the Has Bin, the mind. The limitations of that storage device need not be the promise of the future."

"Should we get rid of the mind, michael? Is it useless?"

"No, Richard, the mind, in its proper place, is a great servant. It is designed to be a storage device, and much like a computer, it is useful for its task. The problem begins when we allow the mind to make our decisions for us, when we allow it to run our lives. You use your computer to store and recall information when you need it, but what would you say to the person who makes no choices for themselves, the person whose computer makes all of their decisions? Might you say to that person: **'Wake up, there is another world out there, another whole level of aliveness. Your computer 'mind' can't think, it can only spit out what has been put into it. Let go of it as your decision making device, make your own choices and take charge of your life!'**

"In the Aramaic creation story Adam goes to sleep. Have you noticed that nowhere do they mention him waking up? The root of the word 'Adam' means 'red clay.' I propose they were telling us we were asleep in the realities that come from the *body's* memory bank and, therefore, stuck in the mind of the past—asleep, so to speak. We are more than a *body* or a mind, we are designed to live in a larger context—the world of actuality. We are not designed to be trapped in the tiny framework of the Adam-mind which only knows how to repeat its past, its *Why Is This Happening To Me . . . AGAIN?!*"

> WE ARE LED TO BELIEVE A LIE
> WHEN WE SEE WITH AND NOT THROUGH THE EYE.
>
> William Blake

> ⚷ KEY THOUGHT—What you are looking for is what is looking.

"There you go again, michael, making perfect sense. I want to hear more! I can't seem to get enough! It feels like every concept, every word is feeding my soul!"

"That is *exactly* the idea of true Spiritual teachings, Richard. They were *Spirit-rituals*. Rituals or tools for realizing our true nature, which is not physical but in the level of energy beyond physical, a level of energy called Spiritual. These tools were created to assist us in waking up from the Has Bin and putting an end to being controlled by the past realities in our minds. They are the keys to awakening and stepping into true aliveness.

"Once a person realizes there is another way to live life and there are *real tools* available for doing Spiritual work, it often *seems* as though nothing else matters. Finding this other way of living, in the Aramaic, was called 'finding the Pearl of Great Price.' It is exciting to catch the vision of a New Self, alive and vibrating with the delight of existence, coming into expression, and the old painful life of the mind passing away. In its roots, this Spiritual process was known as awakening or being reborn—a very real experience."

"You know, michael, when someone asks, 'Have you been reborn?' I usually feel like I am about to be pounced on if I don't answer the way they expect. I feel like I'll be cut off because I'm not part of their 'in crowd.'"

"I think you will find that the person who uses force and becomes obnoxious when asking a question about *being reborn*, is not as reborn as *they* would like to think. Love does not abuse, it gently demonstrates what it has found and holds the space for others to find the gift. Some people also get genuinely enthusiastic, perhaps overly enthusiastic, in their desire to help others find what they have experienced."

"I see that there is another level of meaning to being 'reborn,'" Richard said pensively. "I'm ready to wake up! I want to get this process over with yesterday! Let's do it!" Richard was at another new level of enthusiasm.

"Slow down a little, Richard. If you get ahead of yourself, it will wreak havoc in your life. In the Aramaic, people were warned 'not to storm the gates,' not to go too quickly. Doing your inner work is a process that takes time, and remaining in balance throughout that process makes life much easier," I cautioned. "Each of the tools we offer is designed to assist in keeping that balance. Some people get so excited about the intellectual aspect of this work, they forget to use the tools. Using them is of paramount importance for maintaining balance!

"Some people, on first hearing, have an uncanny understanding of this work and use the tools automatically. For them, it is like recalling something they've always known and wanted. Living in an awakened state is such a radically different way to view life that, while others find that this work rings true for them, it takes more time to make sense of the concepts involved. These people require discipline to use the tools. Still others go through a period of total confusion when they begin this study."

"Which category do you suppose I'll be in, michael?"

"It really doesn't matter, Richard. The key lies in doing your work. **Many people alternate between clarity and confusion each time new levels of understanding and empowerment are reached.**

"Each time you use the tools, new insights will open. Information that was not available the time before will pop into your head," I volunteered.

"Wait a minute," Richard broke in, "that just doesn't make any sense. If the information is there, it is there. It makes sense that it is available no matter when you read it!"

142

"That would seem to be true, but recall our discussion of actuality versus reality. **Reality is the meaning that shows up in your brain, out of the Has Bin, as a result of an actuality you have experienced.** What shows up in your brain comes from what is 'built into brain cells'—not from what you read, or marks on a piece of paper. If information is not in the Has Bin, it cannot be served up to you as a reality."

"Explain to me again what 'built into brain cells' means."

"Information has to be in your structure before your brain can turn it into a reality. Though information may be on a piece of paper, it is not available through your brain as a reality until it is in your brain cell structure.

"What we 'see,' when we 'see,' is the image output from the mind, not what is in the world. Every image seen through the mind is internal to that mind. The physicists tell us that what goes on in the world of actuality is a whirling mass of energy, moving in patterned ways. *The eye cannot 'see.'* It is a frequency device, an antenna, tuned to certain frequencies we call the visible light spectrum. It brings those frequencies into the brain. The mind, a function of brain cells firing, filters everything through its own content. **Anything inconsistent with that content will be changed to conform to the internal belief system of the evidential device, the mind.**"

Richard broke the chain of thought. "I notice I'm not breathing, and I am surprising myself at how often I don't. What surprises me most is that, for as frequently as I hold my breath, I usually don't even know when I'm doing it. For something as basic as breathing, I would think I'd be more aware of it when I'm not!" he gasped. "When I do breathe, michael, all this information feels like overload. It feels like I can't grasp it, I feel stupid," he acknowledged.

"Good!" I replied. "Nice catch! What I hear is that you are noticing for yourself when unconsciousness surfaces, which usually means the Has Bin is having one of its conflicting realities challenged. Holding your breath tends to lock your awareness into the smallness of the mind of the past. Breathing opens the larger context of actuality and is one of the keys to dumping the Has Bin's contents when they are inaccurate or no longer useful.

"Who taught you, who gave you the thought, you were stupid?" I asked. "When a reality like this surfaces, if you stay conscious, it is your opportunity to forgive, to remove that reality from the Has Bin."

"My dad always called me stupid! Are you saying that I took on the reality 'Being Stupid' and now as it surfaces I have the chance to *Forgive*—get rid of that reality in my mind—or be run by it, which you call going unconscious? As I put this together with the Evidential Mind stuff you explained earlier, it occurs to me that if I accept 'Being Stupid' as my reality, my mind can only give me evidence of that and I'll 'be' stupid. Is that why 'Being Stupid' has plagued me all of my life?"

"That's the way it works!" I confirmed.

"I'm changing that thought! I'm letting go of that idea, now!! I've been blocked by the reality of 'Being Stupid' long enough. It has interfered with everything. It's been terrifying, almost like a dragon has been chasing me. Honest! That's what it feels like!

"Hmmm, is this what was meant by 'the casting out of demons?'" Richard asked. "That's what it seems like to me. I bet that was the kind of thing they were referring to in the Scriptures when they spoke of demons. It was getting free of the things that haunted us from out of the Has Bin. They were referring to this inner healing process, right?"

"Exactly. Our disintegrative inner thought complexes are our demons, Richard."

"I'm seeing that, michael. A whole complex of 'Being Stupid' thoughts and feelings just surfaced for me. It felt overwhelming and confusing when that happened, but somehow it was different from when it has happened in the past. Whenever that occurred before,

I would get lost in the feelings and buy into being powerless. Just now I stayed conscious and processed—I think that's what you would call it—through those thoughts and feelings without getting lost in my 'stupid' pattern. This feels great, it feels like relief!"

⊶ KEY THOUGHT—When we lay claim to the "evil" in ourselves, it can be Forgiven. We then no longer need fear its occurring outside of our control.

"Nice work! Yes, this is process and I think you just worked through one of your *demons* or what are sometimes called 'drag–ons' and in some circles, 'Kling-ons.'

"Richard, you are grasping this information quickly and I'm glad you notice it doesn't have to be heavy, it can be fun. It is a process of building brain cells. It takes time to understand this information. As you do this work and 're-view' these ideas, you will grasp new levels of meaning. Your understanding and insights will deepen. Your natural brilliance, the brilliance *we were all created with*, will shine through. Be patient with your learning process!

"Let's look again at the way the mind works. All output must conform to whatever realities have been built into brain cells. Each reality the mind generates must match the pattern of what is in the Has Bin, in the mind's belief system. The mind formulates its output according to the content of brain cells. **The secrets are hidden *by* the mind, not *in* the mind.** It is the mind that 'sees,' and it only 'sees' the images *it* generates. It only generates images for which it has brain cells and meaning."

"What is possible when we get past the insane, the loveless meanings we have been trained into, michael?"

"Richard, who knows, but from the records of Spiritual giants of the past, things are going to be very different. Perhaps there is a 'Garden of Eden' available, but we don't let it enter. Have you ever watched how a child keeps coming back with Love? Perhaps we did not get kicked out of the Garden, but gave up our natural, created condition, Love, by accepting the world of our cultural training, and acting as though the insanities contained in the Has Bin were true.

"Perhaps we will 'see' that **we, the world and everyone in it, deserve to be perceived through the condition of Love just because we each exist.** Perhaps when we follow this *First Law*, we will see the evidence that shows us that *we will benefit* in ways not yet conceived. Love cannot be *taken* away from us, we *push* it away. A fresh perspective is necessary. The mind must be cleansed of insanity, of everything less than Love. A mind that could conceive of actuality free of a past that colors what the Creator created is a mind capable of what was called an 'immaculate conception.'"

> ☞ KEY THOUGHT—Love cannot be *taken* away from us, we *push* it away.

"I hear that you are saying there is a deeper meaning to all of the old teachings, and I'm starting to grasp that they apply in my life. I'm a little blown away."

"This idea of realities being available only if they were built into brain cells was addressed in Aramaic when the Scriptures referred to 'the eyes to see, and the ears to hear,' or, 'having eyes, see ye not? and having ears, hear ye not?' Obviously, the people who heard those words had eyes and ears. However, if they did not have the information in brain cells, though they saw or heard the same words or actions as others, the deeper meanings of the teachings could not show up in their minds. They could not 'hear' or 'see' intended meanings."

Richard broke in, "I'm not sure I understand."

"Are you familiar with computers, Richard?" He nodded. "Let's look at a computer analogy that might help make sense of these ideas."

dr. michael ryce

22

WHAT IS LEARNING?

"Remember when you first sat down at a computer? You had an idea what could be done, but because you had not **built the brain cells** for operating it, you had no realities in your mind to guide you. Therefore, you could not get it to perform. Once you studied computers or an expert helped you build the brain cells, you could run it successfully.

"Prior to being able to operate the computer, the only difference between you and the expert was the content of her brain cell structure compared to yours. She had realities about computers that you had not yet built. Once you developed 'the eyes to see,' you were able to tap the creative capacity of the computer because you now had the brain cells.

"Notice, when the computer wouldn't perform for you, it did not mean there was something wrong with the computer or with you. All the possibilities were there. If you crashed the computer, it was not interested in being vindictive and *punishing* you, it simply did not work the way you wanted it to work. This is a perfect model of what happens in life."

"So, getting the computer to work takes learning. Is that what you call building brain cells?" Richard interjected.

"Yes, and in life we live out the realities for which we have brain cells. Life does not 'punish.' It only gives us back what we ask for. If the realities we hold in brain cells call for what looks like punishment, life will be limited to doing just that, again and again, until *we* change! Just like the computer, when you learn how life works, its creative capacity will open up to you.

"Developing a deeper comprehension of how we learn and refining our understanding of the difference between 'reality' and 'actuality' will make this work easier to grasp. In the Aramaic culture, the distinction between actuality and reality was well understood. **Through the brain, we can only see and grasp a reality that is in our brain cell structure, though we may *think* we see and understand what is happening in the outside world.** There is much more to life than what is seen through our limited senses.

"It takes patience to build brain cells for deeper awareness. It takes time to integrate the ideas presented in this work and for significant change to take place. Those without the brain cells will often wonder why others get excited when using these tools.

"I've seen people become impatient with this work because they want all of the information now, instead of taking the time to go through the learning process. I experience some frustration myself because I would like to teach the whole process in one exhale. It would be wonderful if people could have all the understanding and tools in usable form all at once.

"One of the blocks that tends to slow the process is the conflicting realities people have in their minds about words. The way words are used plays an important part in building brain cells. A word may be understood in various ways, it may be hooked into a variety of realities, individual to each mind. There are agreed upon meanings that *seem* to be inherent in words, but the *only* meaning a word has is the reality it brings up in an individual's brain cell structure. Just because people agree upon a definition does not mean the word itself holds that or any meaning."

"I can see, michael, that just keeping clear on the concepts of reality and actuality will take time for me, but I'm up for the challenge! I can see it is going to involve unlearning old habits of thinking and ingrained behaviors. It's time for me to deal with the things that haven't worked in my life. I just need to get past the feelings that overwhelm me when I think about how much work I have to do.

"I don't agree with everything you have said, and some of it doesn't click for me yet, but I've looked at many other approaches and this one makes more sense than anything else I've investigated." Richard spoke with an unexpected enthusiasm and sincere appreciation.

"Putting these tools to work in your life will fill in many blanks and answer most of your questions. Let's look at the *Forgiveness* process as it is presented in the Reality Management Worksheet," I suggested.

Richard assured me he was willing to do whatever it would take, and for the first time since he arrived acknowledged that he knew this was what he needed. Richard looked calm.

> ○━┳ KEY THOUGHT—Want change?
> Start with the part you control. Your "self."

Notes

dr. michael ryce

23

THE ARAMAIC SOLUTION

"Richard, I feel the 'Reality Management' Sheet is one of the best tools we have developed for cleaning out conflicting realities. **It shows how to *Forgive*, step by step. Once you learn it, if you use it regularly, life will never be the same.**"

"That sounds like a promise I can't refuse. I'm willing!" Richard was enthused. "Tell me more."

"The Aramaic word 'shbag' has been translated into the English word 'forgive,' but it actually has a much deeper and richer meaning than our Western concept of forgiveness. The word itself translates as 'to cancel, to let loose, or to untie.' As an Aramaic concept, the word 'shbag' means a 'tool for changing a reality in your mind.'

> ☙━ KEY THOUGHT—*True Forgiveness*: a tool for changing a reality in your mind.

"In our culture we say 'forgive your brother' as though it is your brother that needs to be forgiven for *your* upset. An Aramaic mind that understood the original teachings on *Forgiveness* would never say such a thing."

"What would they say?"

"The statement would be, '*Forgive* as to your brother.'"

"Wait a minute," Richard broke in as he stood and stretched. "You're losing me."

"Give me a moment to tie it all together, and see if what I'm saying fits. Does it make sense to you to define reality as the output of the mind? Can you accept that we are each responsible for our own realities?"

"Okay, I'm with you so far."

"If I am functioning responsibly and you bring a reality, let's say fear, to the surface for me, is there anything I should be forgiving you for?"

"Well, if I look at it your way, no, because I've just triggered your fear, not caused it. I guess you could say I've given you an opportunity to get rid of that fear," he conceded. "Hey, you know, I've actually given you an opportunity to get rid of something that was hurting you, even though you weren't aware of what was causing pain or dis-ease in you!"

"Exactly. The difference is that when I use the misunderstood form of forgiveness '*to forgive you,*' I must first blame or project onto you. In the Aramaic concept, each person takes responsibility for the content and output of his or her mind. **When you engage in *True Forgiveness* you cancel what you want from your own mind.** Strange as it may sound, this allows your projections to be undone and healing to occur. At first, this is usually a difficult concept to grasp when applied to practical situations because in our programmed experience of the world, it *seems* like it is *other people* who make us feel what we feel. Let's discuss the theory behind why this process works a little later.

"Remember, we defined projection as blaming another for the output of *your* mind? Doesn't it seem a little ridiculous for me to blame *you* for a reality in *my* mind?"

"It does sound strange when you say it that way," he agreed halfheartedly. He paced the floor. "I'm still not convinced. It certainly doesn't feel like I'm projecting when I am upset with someone."

"That is because of the way our minds work, Richard. We have the amazing capacity to make it appear that our internal realities are outside of us. Knowing this, the mind's distortions can be bypassed. As you realized earlier, all healing is an inside job!

"From the Aramaic point of view, your triggering me gives me the needed opportunity to see something inside of myself that needs to be *Forgiven*! I can then *Forgive* 'as to' the reality you bring up in me, but in no way do I need to forgive you.

"Let's look at the Aramaic form of *Forgiveness* as it applies to the scene we discussed earlier when we talked about Blockage of Truth. (Pages 49-53) In the illustration I used in that discussion (Pages 50-51) observe that most of the language in those diagrams we identified as being projection communication.

"In this next illustration (Page-154) take note of the language that each person uses. It comes from our workshop entitled *Communication—Did You Hear What I Think I Said?* and is called 'Responsibility Communication.' Observe that the words they use reflect that they each understand their responsibility for their individual realities.

"In the earlier diagram we did, all of the language was what we call 'projection language,' which is based on the belief that someone else causes our realities and our pain. In that example false forgiveness was used. He 'forgave' her, remember? False forgiveness reinforces the reality in his mind that she is to blame and leaves his internally-produced pain intact."

ARAMAIC FORGIVENESS

"So he shouldn't forgive her?" Richard asked.

"Once you understand *True Forgiveness* as taught in Aramaic you will never 'forgive' another again! **You can't forgive anyone else—*True Forgiveness* has to do with changing the reality triggered in your mind by another, *not letting them off the hook* for doing it.** It is this dynamic and this dynamic ALONE that frees the mind of its hostility and allows us to follow the *First Law* of human existence—the maintenance of the condition of Love. To disobey that Law is to be insane."

"I've made some good decisions when I was angry, michael. I don't know how that fits with what you are saying."

dr. michael ryce

"Richard, each time you get angry do you tend to make similar decisions, even if the resulting behavior does not produce what you want?" He answered yes. "Doing the same thing repeatedly and expecting a different result is a good definition of insanity. If you make the same decision repeatedly, even if it is a good one, choice has not entered the picture. Decisions are the automatic product of resonance and do not lead to new behavior. Have you ever been enraged with someone and spontaneously rushed to embrace and tell them how much you love them? Not likely. That would require unusual circumstances or disciplined choice for most people. Decisions usually do not leave room for new choices or intelligent action and produce what I call an 'insane' mind.

> ☞ KEY THOUGHT—Doing the same thing repeatedly and expecting a different result is a good definition of insanity.

"Recall earlier that I asked when you were most intelligent? You said the only time you had made decisions and done things you regretted was when you were in a state other than Love. Our behavior is only insane when the mind is in the condition of hostility, fear or a reaction to one of those emotions.

"*True Forgiveness* removes from the human system the realities that defile human intelligence, health, prosperity and relationships. It is the key to aliveness."

"How do we do this worksheet process? I don't have a clue what subject to do it on. Do you have any suggestions?"

"Let's explore the waitress picking up your cup of coffee in the restaurant. I think some of the things revealed in that conversation will be useful to discover how your mind produces its *Why Is This Happening To Me . . . AGAIN?!* experiences. It should be fertile ground for finding material for several productive worksheets." (Refer to pages 31-34.)

"I'm ready to look at everything in my life," Richard confided. He seemed inspired to begin the worksheet process.

"Let's look at what your description of the events that day in the restaurant alluded to, and see if any of the issues I think might be there are accurate. For instance, when you were small, were there brothers or sisters that your parents favored over you, perhaps to the point they gave your toys to them?" I probed. "Did you ignore and fight a lot with them?"

"Things were always taken from me, I never had anything to myself—but how do you know that? I don't see how you figured that out." Richard sounded bewildered.

"I didn't know it, but I suspected it when you told me, in rough detail, about the waitress picking up your coffee."

> ⚷ KEY THOUGHT—Your words show you what mind energy you are using to construct your realities, moment to moment.

"I didn't tell you about my childhood then," Richard countered.

I explained to him that "he" didn't, but "his-story" did. Almost everyone experiences their own internal reality in place of what is happening in the world. This means there is a pattern or theme for every reality flowing from brain cells. The words coming from a mind reflect the general patterns contained in the mind of the speaker. Words of delight and inspiration reflect the way life is designed to be, angry words reflect an angry history, sad words a sad past, and fearful words tell the story of a mind brought up in what is perceived as an unsafe world.

"Listening to people speak about *any* reality in their mind gives you a great deal of information about what has happened in their past." We reflected on the idea that the perceptual output of a mind tells you more about the content of that mind than about the object it perceives. "The output of a mind is *always* based on the content

156   dr. michael ryce

of that mind and *may or may not* accurately reflect the external world, the world of actuality."

We reviewed the actualities from that day in the restaurant and the realities Richard's mind fed him. We distinguished between the two. He had experienced the *actuality* of a waitress picking up a cup of coffee. His mind fed him the *reality* from his past that something was being taken away. We discussed the fact that his 'someone's taking something from me' reality surfaced because it was in him to be triggered, not because the waitress took his coffee. His thought that people take things from him was a filter through which he viewed life, and this was his opportunity to use *True Forgiveness* to change that reality in his mind.

He was dismayed and excited, all in one breath. "I didn't know my words made me so transparent and I'm getting a sense of how you figured me out. How did you know I used to ignore my sister and fight a lot?" he asked.

"Recall, you said you attacked the waitress without her having a chance to explain? You would likely attack that quickly only if you had built a reality that says something like, 'Attack first. Don't listen. If you listen, you will lose!' It is a common reality in families where parents play favorites."

"That's painfully close to my relationship with my sister," he admitted. "Why don't you tell me all about me?" he asked.

"You will notice, Richard, that I'm checking out what I'm hearing from you. That is an important step in this process. When I hear your words, I can only hear them for what they trigger in me. **My meaning for your words might be totally off base. The key is, what your words trigger in you, not what they mean to me.** I always work to keep my insights and feedback in the form of questions so *I stay on track.* I'm here to support your looking into *your* issues, *not mine.* I'm not here to 'tell' you anything.

"Words are a topic we could spend hours on, and in some of our intensive workshops we do. A good practice is to observe the words you speak. If you see yourself using words that are not in support of what you truly want to create in your life, use the tools to change your reality structure and your speech.

> **KEY THOUGHT**—What do you believe about yourself to create what is happening in your life? Not sure? Listen to your words for clues!

"Do you have any thoughts about a topic for your worksheet?"

24

WORK-IT-OUT
WITH YOUR BEST FRIEND

"Where do I start?" Richard asked.

"The best place to start is to be clear on what you are doing and why you are doing it. **The people who really *use* these worksheets tell me that they become the best friend they ever had.** Note, the emphasis is on *using* the tool. What the process does is give you an opportunity to confront directly the parts of your mind and life that don't work for you, the parts with which you might sabotage yourself."

"I feel a little resistance to that thought, michael."

"You are not alone, nobody wants to feel their pain—until they understand."

"Understand what?" Richard asked.

"Pain takes its toll even when it is not consciously felt."

"How so?"

"Recall our discussion about pain? Pain is the reflection of stored destructive energies. When people deny and restrict access to pain, the only thing they have accomplished is keeping it out of direct sight. Hidden or anesthetized pain is not *removed* from experience through denial or drugs. It is felt as the aches and pains of so called 'aging,' the twinge of emotional upset that floats in and out of our experience, the irrational outbreaks that destroy relationships, the 'accidents' that occur, headaches and *body* aches, degenerative dis-eases and the thousand irritations that subtract from the possible quality of life.

"There is an old saying that the brave die once, the coward a thousand times. When you are fortified with actual tools to face and heal whatever is hidden, trauma and pain are dismantled and removed from life. As you do this work, you will find your enjoyment of life, your sense of well-being and your aliveness increase in proportion to the amount of *Forgiveness* you do. In the past, if life was lived without tools, most found that facing an old trauma meant reinforcing it and being powerless to change. The *True Forgiveness* process changes all of that. *Shift happens!!* The issues of life can be faced and healed."

"Okay, michael, I see the *why* of doing the Reality Management process, I'm not sure I understand the *what*."

"The *what* is simple. If someone triggers anger, fear, rage, hate, vengeance, gossip or any other dis-integrative reality in you, it is your opportunity to heal yourself—not by letting them off the hook, but by changing the pain producing reality in your mind.

"Whatever your experience of life is, every reality in your mind is changeable. You cannot directly change what happens in the outer world. People become frustrated and uptight when they continuously try to control life. **The way to change the outer world is through indirect influence—by changing the realities in your mind you shift your whole energy field.** When you do, the whole pattern of your life shifts and the *ripple* effect changes everything you attract. If abundance is your issue, *pennies* turn into dollars! The traditional translations of the Scriptures speak of the fall of man. In the Aramaic, that text refers not to a fall, but, instead says, 'man forgot how to live in abundance.' Heal the poverty realities in your mind, whatever the

dr. michael ryce

form of poverty—relationship, money, work, joy, health or abundance—and a change in outer circumstance is pulled in *automatically* through the *Law of Resonance.*"

"Okay, I understand what it is we are about to do. Now I pick a topic? What kind of topics are fair game for a worksheet?"

"You can do a worksheet on any person, place, thing or event that resonates a painful reality in you. It can be a present moment event or something from your past or even a future, anticipated event. You can also use your own emotions or yourself as the subject of a worksheet."

"I could do a worksheet on conflict with women. I've had conflict with my mom, my sister and almost *every* woman with whom I've ever had a relationship, including waitresses!"

"That covers a lot of territory, Richard. I would suggest you be *very specific* and choose a *mildly disturbing* topic for your early worksheets. A narrowly defined subject will produce the best results," I recommended. "Also, *Forgiveness*, like any other skill, is developed through practice. The first time you use this tool, it is best to start with something a little easier than your biggest issue in life. Your lifelong issues tend to have a lot of unconsciousness attached to them, and it is best if you can start with something small enough that you can stay relatively conscious. As you build your strength through doing Reality Management Sheets, you can move to the bigger situations in your life.

"I suggest you keep a journal of your work and an ongoing list of 'worksheets to be done.' You will probably find it productive to do many sheets around your conflict with women."

He was deep in thought before he spoke. "A worksheet on being close to my sister, Amy, might be a good starting point. It seems being close to people is a little less of an issue than conflict with women, though that is still a fairly big issue for me."

"Normally I would suggest you wait until you have used the worksheets for a while before tackling that kind of issue. Since we are doing this together and you have support rather than doing it by yourself, let's go ahead and start by filling out the date and sheet number. (See worksheet form at end of this chapter, page 182-183.)

"I suggest you get a three ring binder and keep your worksheets in it. In the future, each time you look back at old sheets, they will give you new gifts and new insights. *Step 1* on the sheet is about getting clear on the source of your reality. When you start each sheet with this reminder, it is easier to get past your projections of wanting to either blame others or yourself. Blame, aside from a way to give away your power, is an avoidance mechanism."

1. My reality is made with thoughts from my own mind. As I learn to change my thoughts, my reality will change.

"I'm seeing more and more of the Truth of that thought, michael. It is actually starting to feel like an empowering idea. I'm realizing that reality is in my mind and it is changeable!"

"**Step 1A** acknowledges what *seems* to be true and gives you the space to write down your thoughts. If there is not enough room, use another piece of paper. Some people write the entire form out in longhand each time they do a worksheet. In the first blank, in **1A**, you name the person, place, thing or event that triggers your disturbing or painful reality."

"I put my sister, Amy, in this blank?" he asked.

"In this case, yes. If you did a worksheet on, let's say, your car not starting, 'car' would go there. If you were to do a sheet on the idea we processed earlier today, 'being stupid,' that is what you would put in the first blank. Next, you place your own initials between the brackets as a reminder that this worksheet is about *you* and a reality in *your* mind. You then write a brief description of what you perceived as happening."

1A. I seem to be upset because (write the name of the person, thing or situation) *my baby sister Amy* (**R. S.**) **(write what has happened)** *was the favorite.* (BREATHE)

"In the next blank, **1B**, write your feelings. Be sure to use words that describe emotions, not thoughts. You can't feel like 'she was the favorite,' because that is a thought. Sometimes it is difficult to say what your feelings are, and the box on the right is a place to draw and describe them," I offered.

1B. This triggers my feelings of *anger.*

"This is easier than I thought it would be, michael."

"Good, and the next step is a little more of a challenge. The idea with **Step 1C** is to identify the thought you use to cause your feelings of anger."

"I remember we talked about this earlier, but I'm not sure I quite get the idea yet. What does 'identify the thought I use to cause my anger' mean?"

"What thought, specifically, do you have to think in order to be angry about your sister being what you perceived as the favorite?" I asked.

1C. My thought that causes this feeling is *Amy had it easy, I never had it so good!*

"That's a cinch. She had it easy, I never had it that good!" His voice went up a couple of octaves as he spoke. It was clear that his emotions were still right on the edge from the processing we had done earlier in the day. He had accomplished something uncommon for a man in our culture; he became safe enough to be open and vulnerable. "I'm still not quite sure how that thought causes my anger, though," Richard added.

"If you held the thought, 'How sweet, my sister had things so much easier than I did and I'm happy for her!' how would you feel?"

"Delighted, I guess." he answered.

"So, the actuality is the same. The only thing that changes for anger to become delight is the thought *you* think, right? Who suffers from your negative thoughts?" I queried.

"It's getting clearer for me that I'm the one who causes me to suffer and it boggles my mind that I do it so automatically." Richard paused as his thoughts jelled. "You know, michael, I understood this concept about two hours ago when we were talking and was amazed by the whole idea. Now, it's like I'm hearing the idea for the first time. I am understanding how my thoughts generate my feelings all over again, and it amazes me just as much now as two hours ago!"

"I can relate to that, Richard. It amazes me each time I teach it. Life works so differently from the way most of us were trained to think. An important question to ask is, 'Who is in charge of what you think and feel?'"

"In the past it has been everybody but me! I am ready to take charge of my mind and be responsible for the thoughts I think. I'm grasping that my feelings are a result of my thoughts and the words I use. So I guess I'll also start taking full responsibility for them. I'm going to be more careful of the words I use and have more integrity in the way I act. Hopefully, all these things together will improve the results I produce in my life."

"Great! **Step 1D** is pretty straightforward. You simply describe what it is you want to do to punish the trigger in **Number 1A**. Punishment might be anything; a sneer, a degrading thought, leaving, or emotional, verbal or physical abuse."

1D. I want to punish by *yelling and getting rid of Amy.*

"**Step 2** is a reminder that punishment and blame are not your friends, they are a ball and chain. They may bring relief in the short term, but the consequences are always destructive to your physiology, the way your mind works and your happiness!"

"Can a little anger really hurt you that much?" Richard was definitely not convinced.

"I'm not sure how to tell the effects of a 'little' anger, but I suspect if we were to quantify it we would find that anger is one of the major destructive forces to the *body*. We are so good at suppressing, we don't usually have the opportunity to directly confront the effects of our feelings until it is too late and we are facing a major degenerative condition.

"Let's look at **Step 2**, where you acknowledge that:

2. Punishment and blame are not my friends. I now choose to be responsible. ☑

"Remember, the mind always believes it's right. In **Step 3**, it is time to put aside being right and acknowledge that even if you are right, the way you are feeling is self-destructive and it is time to let go of those feelings."

"Wait a minute, michael, this sounds like I have to give in to people even when I know they are wrong. Being a doormat doesn't sound any more appealing than having destructive energies rolling around inside of me."

"Remember, Richard, this is about healing the destructive energies we carry AND holding others accountable for their behaviors. Through *Forgiveness*, we will be able to hold others and ourselves accountable from a clear, functional mind and Loving space that supports relationship rather than creating separation.

"As you fill in the blank with your answers from **Step 1**, check off the boxes and at the same time think the release thought or speak it out loud, if practical."

3. I want to feel better. I let go of my feeling of (1B) _anger_ ☑
and my thought that (1C) _Amy had it easy, I never had it so_
good! ☑ **I let go of my need to be right and punish by (1D)**
yelling and getting rid of her. ☑

"Why would I want to release my thoughts?" Richard asked.

"If you inflict pain on yourself with a thought, you let go of it so you can heal. If there is rage or fear in you as a result of that thought, it is *your* work to heal the rage and fear. Remember, you get the original, she gets the carbon copy. Many of us have been taught we need to be angry to get what we want. In Truth, getting what you want is easier to create from a space of peace and clarity than from a space of anger. You also get to release the stress of the anger held in your *body* and achieve higher states of health and aliveness in the process. Health is not the condition of being free of symptoms. **In this work we define Health as the state of Conscious, Active, Present Love. An absence of that state is dis-ease and the beginning of *all* organic degeneration.**

"Other benefits of letting go of disturbing thoughts are that you will have peace of mind and your mind will no longer need to create scenarios that justify your being angry." He seemed satisfied that these ideas made sense and relaxed more with each step of the worksheet. The resistance that had shown up time and again earlier in the day vanished. I think it was a relief for both of us. Working with someone who is willing certainly is easier.

"***Step 4*** is the act of acknowledging how you want to live. Recall we spoke about the power of words? When word phrases show up with ease in our speech, it tends to be more natural to create those circumstances. The person who uses angry words will tend to easily find circumstances about which to be angry. The person who regularly uses peaceful speech will find peace comes easily. Our words reflect what we are attracting into our lives."

4. I am willing to live peacefully ☑, be happy ☑ and go through the symptoms of healing. ☑

"I recall what you said earlier about the symptoms of healing (Pages 135-136) and I'm willing to do whatever it takes to heal. It seems bizarre that I used to search for trouble purposely! I consciously, or maybe unconsciously, went looking for it! When I think about the language I used to describe myself, women, the *body* and intimate interaction, it is amazing I held a relationship together for even a week. I had no verbal respect for anything."

"Word patterns are structured in our minds at an early age. Becoming conscious of, taking charge and changing those patterns takes intelligence and commitment. A decent, intimate relationship is impossible if the words we use to describe ourselves, the *body*, the opposite sex or our relationships result in degrading feelings. In the Aramaic Scriptures, it was said that he who could rule his tongue was mightier than he who could take a city."

Richard admitted his language had been pretty "raunchy" for most of his life. He was identifying with the idea that his thoughts caused his feelings and decided he was ready to feel better about life, his *body* and those with whom he had relationships. He liked the idea of maintaining the condition of Love in his mind and took a break to do the exercise on restoring the space of Love. (Pages 71-72) He made a commitment to continue that exercise as a daily practice in his life.

"I do feel lighter than I have felt in a long time. I'm relieved. When I think about what is happening in my life, it seems as though I can handle it." He had a slight glow, and it was great to be part of and watch his transformation occur.

"So often, we turn the way we feel over to an outside source. It would be good to rid yourself of that habit. There are lots of people who want to run your mind—the media, advertisers, movies, governments, religious leaders—just about everyone. It's time to take our power back! I recall the words of George Washington

Carver, the man who spawned the peanut industry. He suffered much abuse, yet retained awareness of who was in charge of his mind. His comment on self-control was, 'I will never allow any man to so defile my soul so as to cause me to hate him.'"

"You know, michael, there are a lot of sayings out there about what 'real men' do. It sounds like 'real men' are in charge of their own minds and lives and operate on Love."

"**Step 5** is designed to restore Love to your mind and confirm that you have done it successfully. If hostility or fear remains active you will not be able to see what you Love about a person or situation. **When you can see what you Love, it is because the condition of Love is in your mind. When the condition of Love is in your mind, then you can Love what you see.**"

5. I choose to restore the condition of Love to my mind. Self-test—a Loving thought I have about (1A) is *Amy was my friend and still reaches out to me often.*

He looked a little sad as he processed how he had pushed his sister away. Richard touched into a deep Love for her that had been long since lost in his childhood hostility.

"Take a breath, Richard. Let's go on to **Step 6** where you identify what you want. It is important in this step to make sure you use only words that reflect what you actually want."

"You mean words like 'What I really want is not to be angry at Amy.' Is that an appropriate answer in **Step 6**?" he asked.

"What is it you want? You sound like you are really clear on what you don't want, but the more you don't want it the more powerfully you will create it in your world."

"How so? I don't see what's wrong with what I said."

"It's not a matter of being wrong. Remember, focusing is a creative act and your words reflect what you are creating. **What you focus on is what you create. When you focus on what**

you don't want you create out of avoidance and automatically create what you are avoiding. It does not matter whether you focus on something out of Love or out of hate—if you thought it, you got it!"

"How would you suggest I word what I want, michael?"

"Sounds to me like you want to be Loved and appreciated as much as your sister."

"That's it! That's what I want!" Emotion welled up as he thought about the possibility of actually being loved and appreciated as he said his sister had always been.

6. What I really want is (use positive words only) _to be loved, appreciated and cared for as much as Amy._

Richard agreed that he could see the difference in the energy he was putting out with the two different thoughts about what he wanted. He was particularly impressed by the change in the way he felt as he switched back and forth from what he wanted to his avoidance thought, "I don't want to be angry with Amy."

"I'm amazed as I pay attention," Richard said, "how each of those thoughts affect the way I feel. You said I would be more sensitive to my feelings if I refrained from smoking and drinking coffee. Could there be that much of a shift in my awareness after leaving nicotine and caffeine alone for just a few hours?" he inquired. I let him know that I thought that could make the difference but it was probably a combination of factors, including the fact that he had processed through a lot of emotion and cleared lots of baggage out of his mind today.

"**Step 7** is an acknowledgment of personal responsibility. It is the step of growing out of long-held childhood fantasies and taking responsibility for the output of your own mind. **Only you cause you to feel. Every thought reflects a choice, therefore, every feeling is a choice."**

7. I am not upset at this person, thing, or situation, but at a reality inside of me. If I'm in pain, I'm in error. ☑

"**Step 8** offers the opportunity to distinguish between responsibility and the mind's cheap copy, blame. It's time, Richard, to decide what your source is—blame or Love. Time to look at what really causes your pain and recognize that every reality output from your mind follows a pattern."

"Been there, done that!" he exclaimed. "Blame hasn't worked for me. I'm ready to go another route. I'm ready to use *Forgiveness* to change every pattern."

8. I take responsibility, not blame, for all of my realities. Every reality in my mind is changeable. I now choose to connect with LOVE instead of my upset. ☑

"**Step 9** is the core of the *Forgiveness* process. Write your answer, what you want from **Step 6**, in the blank in **Step 9**. Recall, in Aramaic, the word 'forgive' means to cancel. Can you cancel the people in your life? Can you cancel your life? Can you cancel today? No, but you can *always* cancel what you want out of a situation. Doing this sets up your mind to process through the unconsciousness around your worksheet issue."

9A. I cancel—let go of—my need (6) *to be loved, appreciated and cared for as much as my sister.*

Richard balked a little at doing this. "Why would I cancel what I want? That seems ridiculous, michael. I deserve to have what I want. You said that yourself."

"I agree with you. You *do* deserve to have what you want! I also acknowledge you as a powerful creator. Why haven't you created what you want?"

"I-I don't know," he stammered. "No one has ever cared for me and appreciated me the way I wanted to be. That has always been the problem in my relationships with women—they are affectionate for a while and then become distant. I'm not sure I quite understand it yet, but I cancel my need to be Loved, appreciated and cared for as much as my sister."

"Is it possible, Richard, you acquired that belief when you were a child? Did your actions with women drive them away and is that what caused intimacy to disappear? The result you produce is that you get to prove, over and over again, you are not Lovable!"

Tears were flowing from Richard's eyes as, once again, feelings welled up from deep inside of him. A quiet sob filled the room as he spoke. "Why am I not Lovable? What is wrong with me? It feels like I've never known what it is to feel Loved, so I've become calloused in order not to feel the pain. It seems so deep, like a dark hole that can never be filled."

"Keep breathing," I suggested gently. You are accessing hidden places in yourself, places that your personality structure helps you to keep out of awareness. It is safe to access those places and move what is locked within. Remember to hold the space of Love, that is where the healing happens. In **Step 9B**, you get the chance to ask for assistance in moving through whatever comes to the surface as you forgive."

"What do you mean?"

"There is a power that in Aramaic is called **'Rukha d'Koodsha.' It is defined as an elemental force in the mind that assists you in letting go of your errors and teaches you the Truth.** It literally means the 'force for that which is proper' for us as humans. How about going ahead and asking now for that assistance?" He spoke the next step out loud and then grew very silent.

9B. I ask for help in letting go of my painful reality. ☑ (BREATHE)

"What is happening, Richard? Are you breathing?"

"I'm really feeling sad, overwhelming sadness and loss. At the same time it's a good sadness, if such a thing is possible. It almost feels like being washed. There is energy running through my hands, and my face is a little numb. I'm realizing that when I was a kid, I blamed my sister for how I was treated by my parents. It seems like I've been really unfair to her. I've taken it out on her all my life, and she was just a beautiful little kid. She didn't deserve what I've done to her and what I have continued to do to her all our lives. I've treated her like she was a nobody—the same thing I accused my parents and women of doing to me all my life!"

"Sounds like you could easily turn the abuse you've done to her on yourself. I'd suggest you be aware of that and live the *commitment* of being *Loving, Gentle* and *Respectful* with yourself."

"It doesn't feel like I deserve it. I hate myself. I've been pretty rotten to her." He was in self-pity.

"You've just uncovered your next few worksheets. I suggest you make a note for your journal or fill in **Step 1A** on some blank worksheets. You would benefit from a worksheet on 'deserving,' and on 'being rotten.' I think 'self-pity' would also be a productive topic on which you could do worksheets.

"I invite you to remember that the purpose of delving into these areas of your life is to recognize what you have done to yourself and others with your mind energy. One of the games of the human mind is to always reproduce its patterns and make abuse look like a justifiable action. What I hear is that your reality 'someone is to blame and punishment is in order' has been resonated, and now that you see your sister's innocence, you are about to turn that reality on yourself. Remember, Richard, you are innocent, too.

"In the Aramaic Scriptures, the mind was called 'the Great Deceiver.' It could take any situation and justify projecting its old realities and its patterns on whatever happens. The task at hand is to bring Love into your mind and heal your tendency to abuse *yourself or anyone else.*

"Do you see how the mind sets its trap? It is urgent in any healing circumstance to have a Law by which you act, a guidepost for decisions and behavior, or you will tend to fall into the trap of the mind. The Law to use is that of Love. You can't listen to the advice of an insane mind and make healing decisions."

Richard was dismayed. "I'm not insane right now, I'm just angry at myself."

"Recall the definition of insanity we discussed earlier? An insane mind is a mind without the condition of Love. The *First Law* is to keep that condition in your mind, whomever you think about, whatever happens! Your focus is on you right now, and you are ready to punish yourself for the error of a child who was in pain. You didn't understand what happened when a new baby came into your home—how could you? I would suggest you go back to **Step 8** and reconnect your mind to Love before you take any other actions."

"Okay, I really want to get through this. It seems like such a waste, the way I've been with my sister for so many years."

"Great catch. Notice your words. Sounds like another good worksheet topic is 'wasted relationships.' It would be a good idea to make a note of that on your future worksheet list. Have 'wasted relationships' shown up anywhere else in your life?"

"Let me take just a minute and get centered in that Love connection, michael."

We sat silently for a moment and Richard's countenance changed. He seemed to settle a little and then spoke. "It feels as though *every* relationship I've ever had was a waste and I can see that I made the decision very early that relationships weren't safe. The Truth is, I think, that I wasn't safe. I've been so angry ever since I was a child. I'd snap at anybody for what appeared to be no reason. I now see clearly that I was hurting and wasn't going to let anyone get close enough to do it to me again! I can see my life drama is to be emotionally aloof and unavailable just as described in *The Celestine Prophecy*. It is clear that my attitude guaranteed I would be hurt over and over. The old saying, 'There are none so blind as those who will not see,' keeps coming to my mind. I've sabotaged my whole life!"

"Keep your breath open. You still have lots of life left. Let's tie what just came to the surface back to some of our earlier discussions. Recall you said the women in your life were warm and Loving at first, and then they became distant. You then found you couldn't seem to get close to them again. I realize your thoughts made it look like it was all them, but was that projection? Notice your thoughts earlier were that *they* became distant. It sounds like it is you who becomes distant and then blames it on them."

Richard swelled with emotion again. "I can't believe what I've done—and I've beat everyone else up for what I've been doing to them all my life. I don't know if I can handle this."

"There is nothing to handle. *True Forgiveness* is not something *you* do. You simply open the door, and if you allow it to remain open Love does the rest. Just breathe and the energy will move. Remember—healing happens!" Several moments passed as Richard went through waves of emotion.

"What do I do with all of these feelings?"

"Just be with them. It is safe to feel everything inside you. Your job is to open the door and hold the space. Think of our earlier definition of processing. It is the capacity to hold *Love Conscious, Active* and *Present* when anything less than Love surfaces. **You've gotten in touch with some of the issues that your mind hides. You opened the space for that to happen when you canceled or *Forgave* your need for what you wanted. This is *the result of True Forgiveness*!**

"By canceling, you allowed the file in your mind that kept issues hidden from your awareness to open. When these issues surfaced and were exposed to Love, the Truth became available to you and you began to let go—heal—these long-held painful realities. This is how healing looks! You will no longer have to carry these burdens. Your life will change as a result of the process you just went through. I stress, as strongly as I can, that this is the effect of canceling your need for what you want, which is the key to opening the whole healing process!"

Richard regained his composure. "Where did that come from? I didn't expect such a powerful upheaval. Do I feel relieved! I'm going to think about this for a long, long time. I don't know what to say, I'm a little embarrassed."

"Sounds like another worksheet. I support you in letting go of embarrassment. What you just went through is right on target. It's what our culture inhibits us from doing, especially as men— looking at, feeling and dealing with the insanity we go through in life. Our culture has warned us not to open 'Pandora's Box,' but they did not tell us that if we never look into and clean out Pandora's Box our lives will become like its contents. Can you see how the theme of what you have just uncovered has run through your whole life?"

"It has not run *through* my whole life, michael, it has *run* my whole life. That experience and the decisions I made to protect myself from getting hurt again have been at the root of *every* relationship interaction I have ever had! I'm ready to re-create my life differently. It *is* safe to Love and I'm going to do it! Nothing can stop me now!"

"Richard, I might suggest you look at the words, 'Nothing can stop me now.' Recall the discussion about creating out of avoidance? What your words just said is that you are getting ready to set something up to stop you."

"Don't be so literal. That's not what I meant."

"I know that's what you believe but your words reflected avoidance, and your words always precede your creations. At this moment it sounds like I'm being picky, but I'm reflecting back to you where your reality structure is taking you. Your words are the indicator. Words reflect the energies with which we *organ-ize our bodies and our world.* You've just had a powerful opening and insight, but there is still work to be done. Might I suggest you rephrase your intention to something such as, '*It is safe to Love and I'm going to do it! Everyone, including myself, supports me in having Loving, connected relationships, especially with women and particularly with my sister!*'

"In the Aramaic, you have just been born into a new kingdom, a new level of insight. It is exciting, but you have a whole genetic and life history that is going in another direction. Your mind has a store of realities that is inertia bound. Your reality structure will tend to keep you going in its direction, rather than this new way, as soon as it's back in the driver's seat. Your words indicate it is sneaking back in already, and that is as it should be."

"What do you mean 'as it should be'?! I don't want to go back to that old way. I'm ready to move on. I like this new way of thinking and being, and I can hardly wait to tell everyone I meet about it!"

"Be aware that not everyone is going to want to hear what you have to say. Recall when you first called me you thought it would be a waste of time to get together? Remember the 'don't storm the gates' warning? Just be aware that you have work to do and the

Forgiveness process has just begun. There will be other layers of this and other old realities based on the childhood experience you just uncovered that are still to come forward for healing. Those old realities will attempt to convince you they are true, but only because that is what you have trained them to do."

"I'm committed! What do I do?" Richard beamed.

"First, I suggest a commitment of five *written* worksheets a day for the next forty days. As you have just observed, the worksheets put you in touch with your unconscious dynamics. They initiate healing. In the Scriptures, the unconscious is called the 'desert' or the 'heart.' Forty days in the desert is very powerful. Recall in the Scriptures they said, 'Take care the heart for out of it are the issues in life'? Notice how the unconscious dynamic just uncovered has set up the issues in your life."

"It's pretty clear to me right now, but doesn't this put an end to it? I mean we already did a worksheet on this issue. Shouldn't it be over?" Richard asked hopefully.

"No, it's not usually that easy, but it is possible. The *Master Teacher* of the *True Forgiveness* process suggested it might require seventy-seven times seventy worksheets to clear up any given issue. In the Scriptures, seven is the number of completion and a zero added to that number is infinity. This means that you may do an infinite number of worksheets until you are complete with an issue. The real work begins now!

"Transforming all of the old dynamics in the mind is a process that takes time. Recall there are years of old experiences, and generations of beliefs and insane interactions to overcome—aeons of what was called 'wandering in the desert.' This work is the core of the Scriptural teaching that was veiled and available only to those who had the 'eyes to see and the ears to hear.'"

"I didn't know what I was getting myself into, michael, but I'm glad I came. I'll do my work and teach it to others."

"Great! Once you realize what there is to be done, what else is there to do? Let's cover the **last step** on the Reality Management Sheet and we can close for now."

"I want to be at the support team intensive next summer. How do I arrange that?"

"Let's talk about that later and look at **Step 10**, which you've already done, then complete **Step 11**."

10. I now feel *many different emotions; feel cleansed and relieved* **and I can see that** *my sister didn't deserve my hostility and neither did I. I can see that I have lots of work to do and it's safe to look inside me and feel my feelings.*

"It feels like I could write a novel on the insights that are coming from the few hours of work we have done and this one worksheet. Where does it stop? I didn't believe anything so powerful could ever happen to me."

"Writing a book on your work today is a great idea, Richard! I remind you that what you have done is a process and there are highs and lows. When lows come remember the thought, 'This too shall pass,' and it will; it can take up to three days if you do your work. I would suggest you put everything you are thinking into a journal and keep rereading it. It will be fertile ground for future insights and worksheet topics.

"In the **final step** of the Reality Management Sheet, you purposely look for the Love in the subject of your sheet and focus on what you want to create with them. Be clear that your focus is on exactly what you want from the situation."

11. I join with the LOVE in you (1A) *Amy* **and I'm willing to have** *a close, warm relationship with you and to be emotionally available. I will communicate honestly with you and be responsible for what comes up in me.* ☑ **(BREATHE)**

"Relief and hope are what I feel now. It seems I've learned so much about myself—more than I've learned in my whole lifetime! What can I do for you, michael?"

"Richard, there is a principle in physics called critical mass. It is the threshold point where a seemingly small action transforms a large mass. Without charge to the sponsor, we accept every invitation possible to speak to groups. We present our travel workshops free and invite people to copy and give away our materials so that our work is available without regard to the ability to pay. We do these things as our contribution to creating critical mass with these tools.

"Doing your work and sharing it with others will add energy to our family's commitment to deliver these tools to every mind on the planet and is the greatest gift you could give us. We also invite you to support this work financially or in any other way you can. There is always work to be done at *Heartland* and the donation of materials and/or labor is always welcome. Of course, doing and passing on the work is most important.

"I believe a precious opportunity was missed two thousand years ago to heal a suffering, wounded humanity. It was our chance to regain our sanity, our dignity, and to function again as human beings. Recalling that *Love of Truth* is the healer of blockage of Truth, I trust its transforming power. I believe that each mind wants to and will shift to the most rewarding way of living possible, once the possible is seen. The question is who will break through to the critical mass, who will make the possible available to humanity? Consider the following story by an unknown author."

Will You Make the Difference?!

"Tell me the weight of a snowflake," a hawk asked a wild dove. "Nothing more than nothing," was the answer. "In that case I must tell you a marvelous story," said the hawk. "I sat on the branch of a fir, close to its trunk. It began to snow. Not heavily, not a raging blizzard, no, just like in a dream, without any violence. Since I had nothing better to do, I counted the snowflakes settling on the twigs and needles of my branch. Their number was exactly 3,741,952 when the next snowflake dropped onto the branch—'nothing more than nothing' as you say—and the branch broke off." Having said that the hawk flew away.

The dove, since Noah's time an authority on peace, thought about the story for a while and finally said with resolve, **"PERHAPS ONLY ONE PERSON'S VOICE IS LACKING FOR PEACE TO COME ABOUT IN THE WORLD."**

"Richard, the next time someone resonates a reality less than Love in your mind, will yours be the voice for peace?"

dr. michael ryce

EPILOGUE

Dear Reader,

The purpose of each tool in this book and our work is to support the *healing of ourselves, each other and the planet.*

People from many nations are working with and supporting these tools. Will you join with our International *Heartland* family in being *response-able,* using the tools and perhaps become *the voice* that will bring peace and healing to the world?

If anger or upset *in any form* play a part in your relationships or life, will you choose to be a voice for peace?

Blessings,

michael, marijo,
michael jay and christa joy

REALITY MANAGEMENT
NO FAULT EMPOWERMENT TOOLS

Date: _Oct 23_

Sheet Number: _1_

1. My reality is made with thoughts from my own mind. As I learn to change my thoughts, my reality will change.
    A. I seem to be upset because *my trigger* (write the name of the person, place, thing, or event)_ my baby sister Amy _ (R.S.) is (write what has happened)_ was the _ _ favorite _ **(BREATHE)**
    B. This triggers my feelings of_ anger _

    C. My thought that causes this feeling is_ Amy _ _ had it easy. I never had it so good! _
    D. I want to punish by_ yelling and getting rid _ _ of Amy _

Draw your feelings:

2. Punishment and blame are not my friends. I now choose to be responsible. ☑ **(BREATHE)**
3. I want to feel better. I let go of my feelings of (1B)_ anger _and my thought that (1C)_ Amy had it easy. I never had it so good! _ I let go of my need to be right and punish by (1D) _yelling and getting rid of her_
4. I am willing to live peacefully ☑, be happy ☑ and go through the symptoms of healing. ☑
5. I choose to restore the condition of Love to my mind. ☑ Self-test—a Loving thought I have about (1A) is_ Amy was my friend and still reaches out to me often _
6. What I really want is (use positive words only)_ to be loved, appreciated and cared for _ _ as much as Amy _
7. I am not upset at this person, thing or situation, but at a reality inside of me.
    If I'm in Pain, I'm in error.
8. I take responsibility, not blame, for all of my realities. Every reality in my mind is change-able. I now choose to connect with **LOVE** instead of my upset. ☑ **(BREATHE)**
9. A. I cancel—let go of—my need (6) _ to be _ _loved, appreciated and cared for as much as_ _my sister_

    Draw your feelings now:

    B. I ask for help in letting go of my painful reality. ☑ **(BREATHE)**
10. I now feel_ cleansed, relieved _and I can see that_ neither of us deserved my hostility & I have work to do_
11. I join with the **LOVE** in you (1A) _ Amy _ and I'm willing to have_ a close, warm relationship _ _with you & be available—be responsible for my feelings _ with you. ☑ **(BREATHE)**

Photocopy Suggestion: Use enlargement setting of 115% for 8½x11 paper.

REALITY MANAGEMENT
NO FAULT EMPOWERMENT TOOLS

Date:_____

Sheet
Number:____

1. My reality is made with thoughts from my own mind. As I learn to change my thoughts, my reality will change.

A. I seem to be upset because *my trigger* (write the name of the person, place, thing, or event) _____ (__.__.) is (write what has happened)_____
_____ **(BREATHE)**

B. This triggers my feelings of_____

C. My thought that causes this feeling is_____

D. I want to punish by_____
_____

Draw your feelings:

2. Punishment and blame are not my friends. I now choose to be responsible. ❑ **(BREATHE)**

3. I want to feel better. I let go of my feelings of (1B)_____ and
my thought that (1C)_____ I let
go of my need to be right and punish by (1D) _____

4. I am willing to live peacefully ❑, be happy ❑ and go through the symptoms of healing. ❑

5. I choose to restore the condition of Love to my mind. ❑ Self-test—a Loving thought I have about (1A) is_____

6. What I really want is (use positive words only)_____
_____

7. I am not upset at this person, thing or situation, but at a reality inside of me.
If I'm in Pain, I'm in error.

8. I take responsibility, not blame, for all of my realities. Every reality in my mind is change-able. I now choose to connect with **LOVE** instead of my upset. ❑ **(BREATHE)**

9. A. I cancel—let go of—my need (6) _____
_____

Draw your feelings now:

B. I ask for help in letting go of my painful reality. ❑ **(BREATHE)**

10. I now feel_____and I can see that_____

11. I join with the **LOVE** in you (1A)_____ and I'm willing to have_____
_____ with you. ❑ **(BREATHE)**

Photocopy Suggestion: Use enlargement setting of 115% for 8½x11 paper.

Index

dr. michael ryce

Index

dr. michael ryce

HEARTLAND RESOURCE GUIDE

DO YOU WANT TO KNOW MORE?

For those who wish to explore the tools presented in this book, the following resource guide explains the facilities at our teaching center, *Heartland*. In the following pages there is a listing that describes audio and video tapes, workshops, telephone support, written information and children's materials available. An order sheet is included for our mutual convenience.

OUR COMMITMENT?

This Spiritual work belongs to The Creator. Our commitment is to make these tools easily and universally available, regardless of ability to pay. We offer travel workshops free and in order to support our continued work ask a minimum exchange for intensives, tapes and other products. Our mission is the healing of ourselves, each other and the planet and everything we offer is dedicated as our contribution toward that purpose.

Please join in empowering us through your LOVE, donations, tape and book purchases and by attending intensives at *Heartland*. We exchange our intensives and products for any form of needed property, labor or a post office money order.

The Heartland Retreat Center

Heartland is a self-healing retreat nestled in the peaceful Ozark Mountains. Intensives held here are a wonderful opportunity for learning the tools michael and his family teach and for providing support in the practical application of this work in your life.

With a swim dock on Bull Shoals Lake and surrounded by a forest of oak, dogwood and cedar trees, this beautiful environment abounds with deer and wildlife. There are opportunities for hiking, swimming, campfires, the music of flutes, and gardening.

- Gourmet, well-balanced vegetarian meals prepared with the highest quality ingredients. Powerful nutrition increases vitality and enhances the ability to process, one of the major goals of *Heartland*.

- Our cozy cabins offer assorted accommodations. Some space is designated for camping and we have limited motor home facilities.

- Private sessions and group support in the self-healing process are available. We are also here to assist you in acquiring new food habits and making lifestyle changes. Join us!

- Enjoy nature walks and swimming in Bull Shoals Lake, bird watching, campfires, gardening, music making, mountain biking on back country roads or just lazing on the patio or in a hammock soaking up the natural beauty.

The assistance of a dedicated Support Team make *Heartland* intensives a powerful, safe retreat for self-discovery and self-healing.

What Happens
In A Heartland Intensive?

The goal of the *Heartland Intensive Program* is to support participants in expanding their self-healing experience and knowledge. Two things you can expect to experience at *Heartland* are a deepening ability to use each of the tools michael and his family teach and also the completion of a large piece of your inner work. Our travel workshops are taught in an information format with the goal of providing the best information possible and an experience of the particular tools taught in that workshop. *Heartland Intensives* are experiential, process-oriented workshops designed to support you doing your inner work and strengthen your skills.

Those who attend any of these workshops report benefits such as significantly improved relationships, finances, eating habits and freedom from many addictions. Many say their energy levels soar, their mental functioning and emotional stability are enhanced and their bodies trim 10-25 pounds or more.

At *Heartland* we do a variety of intensives that last anywhere from nine days to the three and one-half month Support Team Program. The Team Program is an apprenticeship / work / study session where participants operate the center and participate at least once in each workshop taught during the summer. For more information see the workshop descriptions that follow and the "What People Are Saying" section inside the front cover of this book.

Intensives are an important part of learning to share these *Tools* with others. A Teacher Training and Certification is available for those who want to teach this work. For a current schedule, contact:

Intensive Coordinator
c/o Rt. 3 Box 3280
Theodosia, MO 65761
417-273-4838
whyagain@kcmo.com

AN INTENSIVE EXPERIENCE...

In each intensive that lasts 9 days or more and 17 days or less, Workshops 1-9 will be covered.

(Workshops marked with ** are or will be available on audio cassette.)

1. WHY IS THIS HAPPENING TO ME . . . AGAIN?!**

An original, unique synthesis of science, psychology and theology that is rich with insights from the ancient Aramaic language and culture. Tools are presented for self-healing, putting an end to recurring life patterns and recreating life! *(available in book and on audio and video cassette)*

2. COMMUNICATION–DID YOU HEAR WHAT I THINK I SAID?**

Open mutual support and communication in your relationships. See with clarity the detrimental effects of "projection communication" and grasp the simple shift required to enter the safety and effectiveness of "Responsiblity Communication." In this workshop a system for becoming conscious of and changing life patterns is presented. Open doors to resolve issues, free up creativity and bring higher levels of aliveness into relationships. *(check availability before ordering)*

190

3. ON CREATING CONSCIOUSLY -
KEYS TO AN ABUNDANT LIFE**

A dynamic process for getting clear on what you want and letting go of what you don't want. Break down negative money myths and blocks to receiving. Attitudes we hold that create our conditions in life are investigated. Significant shifts in achieving wealth in all areas of life, relationships, health and finances happen in this workshop.

4. HEALING THROUGH RELATIONSHIPS**

How to form, on a practical level, relationships that nurture and heal rather than reinforce conflict. A workshop focused on learning usable relationship skills. Move through guilt and fear and experience the empowerment connected relationships bring!

5. PURPOSE, PERSONAL POWER AND COMMITMENT**

An empowering workshop that brings insight and clarity to your life's purpose. Learn to align thought and spiritual awareness for personal power. Discover the unique purpose you were created to accomplish. When aligned with your purpose, everything changes! Be "on purpose" and watch your creative capacity explode! *(check availability before ordering)*

6. OPENING THE ENERGY FIELD

A "hands-on" experience of aligning and opening the body's "antenna" to provide a greater energy flow that brings deep, profound relaxation and enhances the ability to release. This is a key part of the *StillPoint Breathing* process.

7. STILLPOINT BREATHING

Experience the power of the breath to uncover past conditioning and remove limited realities. A gentle self-help tool that leads to the direct experience of *Source Connectedness,* self-acceptance and an ever deepening serenity.

191

8. T'AI CHI CHIH

Learn a series of slow, soft movements that help to circulate energy throughout the *body*. According to many practitioners, T'ai Chi Chih produces relaxation, creates more energy, and improves physical and mental health. When done regularly, many report weight loss, increased joint movement, blood pressure reduction and greater mental clarity. Based on ancient healing principles, this easy to learn art form can be done by anyone. *(available soon on video with marijo*)*

9. THE LIVE-IT DIET

Growing and preparing live raw foods is a skill you will achieve. Spiritual, physical, mental and emotional changes occur more rapidly if the *body* is nutritionally sound. Our food is geared to promote nutritional vitality in order to reap maximum benefits from each phase of the intensives. We follow the principles of the Hippocrates program, a step beyond "Fit For Life." See any of Ann Wigmore's books for details.

10. WHY IS THIS HAPPENING TO ME . . . AGAIN?!
TEACHER TRAINING and CERTIFICATION

If you want to deepen your understanding and experience of Forgiveness, the Reality Management Process and/or you wish to teach this work, this is the workshop for you. Once each year a five day segment is added on to the nine day intensive (workshops 1-9). In these extra five days the whole time is spent immersed in the principles of the *Why Is This Happening To Me . . . AGAIN?!* workshop. Spend 14 days with us in this practicum on learning and teaching the core tools presented in this work. If you register for the forty day intensive, you will automatically be included in this segment.

Intensives that last from 18 days to 40 days include
a deepened form of workshops 1-10 and workshops 11-14

11. EMPOWERED TO HEAL**

What is the cause of health? What are the internal conditions that enhance healing? Are there universal principles of healing? Did the Aramaic culture possess keys to wisdom and sound life/mind management lost in "modern" times? Explore the "Be-Attitudes," the powerful, practical, life-transforming revelations from the Aramaic Sermon on the Mount.

12. CO-DEPENDENCE TO INTER-DEPENDENCE**
Survivor or victor? What is the gift of the co-dependent relationship? This segment uncovers the cause of addiction, how to eliminate dependency and create intimacy in the process! Identify and heal "Power Person" issues at the root of our personality and Reality Formation Systems. When denial is removed, conscious relationships provide a forum for recovery. Transform dysfunction into health and wholeness! *(check availability before ordering)*

13. GETTING THE STRESS YOU NEED**
What causes stress? What is appropriate stress and how do you get it? Learn tools to remove damaging stress and get the stress you need!! The stages of destructive stress are: alarm, resistance, adaption fatigue and finally exhaustion (chronic fatigue). Dis-ease and death are signals of the final stages of *unmanaged* stress. Learn how to increase performance in all areas of life by freeing yourself of the burden of useless stress! *(check availability before ordering)*

14. INTUITIVE DEVELOPMENT
According to Albert Einstein, his work was 90% intuition and 10% intellect! We will spend at least five days of the workshop on achieving the ability to gain information without recourse to reason—a direct experience of using the spiritual faculty of intuition!

15. WHY IS THIS HAPPENING TO ME . . . AGAIN?! WORKWEEK
This work / study program is a wonderful way to support *Heartland* improving its facilities. If this work has benefited you and you want to give something back, come and join us for Workweek! It is also an economical way to visit *Heartland* and be steeped in the tools michael and his family teach. In the evenings, the teaching will focus on the principles taught in the "WHY..." workshop. By day, teams will work to accomplish projects on the *Heartland* property. Opportunities will arise to use healing tools in real life situations with people who are committed to healing themselves, each other and the planet. Each afternoon, there will be time to take nature walks, swim in beautiful Bull Shoals Lake or just relax in the fresh Ozark air.

(Workshops marked with ** are or will be available on audio cassette.)

LAWS OF LIVING INTENSIVE

✓ **Ready for a new direction or tools for your life and relationships?**

✓ Just as great minds throughout the ages have applied Scientific Laws to improve life's circumstances so can we, by a study of the *Laws of Living,* learn to manage aspects of life previously thought to be unalterable.

✓ Perfect compliment to the *WHY IS THIS HAPPENING TO ME . . . AGAIN?!* work. This intensive includes *StillPoint Breathing.*

✓ Gain support and heal core issues! A participant's letter says, *"In the class I broke through a childhood situation I now see effected my relationship with my wife and blocked my children out. We now thrive together! Thanks!"* Tim Jordan, St. Louis, MO

✓ 25 years of successful application in the areas of health, mental health, character improvement, business, marriage relations, abundance, substance abuse, delinquency and crime prevention. *The tools work!*

✓ Over 10,000 participants—70-90% *positive personality changes!*

✓ Experience the keys to optimal function and happiness.

This workshop is a minimum 13 day intensive and includes teaching certification. It is often taught as a part of the forty day intensive. "*LOL*" is a practical course, the result of 55 years of combined research and development. It synthesizes and integrates deep insights from the fields of law, science, psychology, neuropsychology, naturopathic medicine, nutrition, theology and especially the *Aramaic* language and culture.

LOL identifies the source of and offers solutions for tension, stress, fear, anger, depression and guilt. It teaches how to improve the way words, intentions, perceptions, goals and decisions effect attitudes and behavior. It shows how motivation works, how to forgive, how to set Loving goals, and how to maintain the condition of Love in the mind. This is an experiential course that includes approximately 225 pages of text material.

SUPPORT TEAM SUPERINTENSIVE

Do you want to enhance your own process, learn our tools and be a part of delivering them to every mind on the planet? This extended program is for those who want to deepen their understanding of this work and establish a strong foundation in the practice of the tools offered in the intensives and/or teach this work. The Superintensive is an excellent way to heal persistent life-inhibiting patterns, establish clear goal setting for one's own life and practice teaching these tools. In the Loving, Safe and Creative space of *Heartland*, you'll develop friendships and strong bonds that will last a lifetime.

Team members support *Heartland* in such areas as office and publicity, building projects and facility maintenance, recreational activities coordination and development, food services, public outreach programs and workshop activities. Support team members receive the benefit of the full range of topics offered in the various intensives for the season and the powerful experience of living these tools in real-life situations. Certification in *StillPoint Breathing, Why Is This Happening To Me . . . AGAIN?!* and *Laws of Living* will be available to each team member. Only for the Self-Response-Able and those willing to learn.

195

Announcing

Heartland Helpline

WHAT IF...
...the support you needed was just a phone call away?

Now you can have the personal guidance and powerful support of two wonderful people! Julie and Kim Haverstick travelled a year teaching with myself and marijo. Together they have over 20 years experience in working with the tools we have developed. Julie has 2 degrees in teaching and has taught school for 24 years. Over the years, she has developed a method for working with these tools with children and has written a book, describing her research. I think her book, *Could This Child Really Be Mine,* is destined to be a best seller.

Kim has a B.A. in finance and has been a self-employed building contractor for 25 years. He possesses a gentle power in the way he teaches this work. Kim and Julie probably hold the record for using the tools to work through issues as a couple and with the world at large. The strongest support you can receive is from someone who willingly walks their talk!

Call if you need support in your process or require assistance in the following areas:
- ✓ Instruction on the Reality Management or Advanced Reality Management Worksheets.
- ✓ Experience one to one support.
- ✓ Want to use Responsibility Communication, My Commitment or Mind Shifters.
- ✓ Awareness of Regulatory Speech and how this supports your core beliefs and repeating life patterns.
- ✓ Gain insights about how to create a Loving, Holy Relationship in marriage.

For assistance and continued education with dr. michael ryce's tools, call Kim and Julie for rates and to schedule a phone appointment.

Helpline information 800-583-9827

michael

WHO AM I?

I am somebody!

I am bright, capable, and lovable.

I am teachable and learn easily.

I tell the Truth and am a gentle listener.

I respect myself and others.

I am cooperative and responsible

for my feelings and choices.

I see the highest and best in myself

and others and support that

with my thoughts, words and actions.

I use time wisely because it is valuable.

I am the best me I can be each day.

I am somebody!

I AM LOVE

My Promise

♡   I promise to tell you the truth
and treat you LOVINGLY, Gently and with
Respect in my thoughts, words and actions.

♡   Being connected to LOVE and
being friends with you are always
the most important things to me.

♡   If I'm not feeling Loving, I will hold us
in my heart as we each gently
talk about our own feelings.
This way, we learn to cooperate
and be responsible for our realities
and help each other change
the ones we don't like.

"Stepping Beyond" Audio Tape Titles
by dr. michael ryce

The following list of tapes is offered on a variety of topics. Most of these tapes are approximately 75-90 minutes in length. Selections by number can be made on the order sheet at the end of this section.

1. Setting The Scene
2. In My Defenselessness
3. The Ego *Body* Illusion
4. The Choice for Completion
5. Creation and Communication
6. Higher Communication
7. Doing Your Work
8. The Rewards
9. Spiritual Awareness
10. Responsibility for Sight
11. Healing and Wholeness
12. Cause and Effect
13. Beyond Perception
14. What You See Is What You Are
15. Right Teaching—Right Learning
16. Key to the Inner Guide
17. The Last Judgment
18. Listening to the Voice
19. Ego and False Autonomy
20. Forgiveness—Key to Happiness
21. Sympathy and Criticism
22. Ideas Leave Not Their Source
23. Two Ways of Perceiving
24. The Illusions of the Ego
25. Pyramid Prophecy
26. Function of the Miracle Worker
27. Perception and Knowledge
28. Relationships
29. Creation by Focus of Consciousness
30. Love and Responsibility
31. Peace of Soul
32. On Creating Consciously
33. Holy Relationships
34. Personal Action Brings World Unity
35. Grievances into Miracles
36. Purpose and Function
37. The Essence of Miracles
38. Let Me Recognize the Problem
39. The Two Emotions
40. Body/Mind—A Trap or Learning Tool
41. Right Use of Judgment
42. Looking at the Ego
43. Ego and the Divided Mind
44. Creating Vs. Self-Image
45. By Grace I Live
46. The Meaning of Easter
47. Healing Our Planet
48. Transition Into Awareness

Heartland Resource Products

Title (All works by dr. michael ryce unless otherwise stated)	Type/Number/Description	Price	Quantity	Sub Total
Why Is This Happening To Me . . . AGAIN?! In harmony with our family's commitment to make these tools available to every mind on the planet, a case of 60 books can be ordered at 6.00 per book—60% off of retail—Total 360.00 plus 20.00 S&H. If you have benefited from and wish to support this work, you might consider giving books as gifts.	4 Hour Audio *See page 190*	40.00		
	4 Hour Video " " "	100.00		
	Book NEW! Based on the *"Why..."* workshop. Includes instructions for Reality Management Sheet. Introduction by James Redfield, *author of The Celestine Prophecy*	15.00		
Healing Through Relationships	4 Hour Audio *See page 191*	40.00		
On Creating Consciously - Keys To Abundance	4 Hour Audio " " 191	40.00		
Empowered To Heal	4 Hour Audio " " 192	40.00		
Communication—Did You Hear What I Think I Said?	4 Hour Audio NEW! * *Check availability* " " 190	*40.00		
Purpose, Personal Power and Commitment	4 Hour Audio NEW! * *Check availability* " " 191	*40.00		
Co-dependence to Interdependence	4 Hour Audio NEW! * *Check availability* " " 193	*40.00		
Getting the Stress You Need	4 Hour Audio NEW! * *Check availability* " " 193	*40.00		
Single Tapes - 75-90 minute selections.	Tape #(s)_____ , _____ , _____ , _____ " " 199	10.00		
12 Tape Package	# 1-12, 13-24, 25-36, or 37-48 " " "	100.00		
36 Tape Package	# 1-36 " " "	250.00		
48 Tape Package	# 1-48 " " "	325.00		
MY COMMITMENT *(see back cover)* by michael and marijo **or 7 for 5.00, 15 for 10.00 for any combination of these items	15 oz Porcelain Mug *See page 197* 5 x 7 Greeting Card, suitable for framing 8 x 10 Parchment, " " " **My Promise** 8 x 10 **My Commitment** or **My Promise** Bookmarks	8.00 **1.00 **1.00 **1.00 **1.00		
I Am Somebody by Julie Haverstick NEW! **or 7 for 5.00, 15 for 10.00 for any combination of these items	Small Poster(8½ x 11) or Bookmark *See page 197* Mug Large Poster	**1.00 5.00 5.00		

Item	Price	Notes
Could This Child Really Be Mine? Book by Julie Haverstick	20.00	
Simplified method of teaching self-discipline, self-healing & empowerment to children at school and home.		
Be-Attitudes (The Aramaic Translation)	2.00 / 3 for 5.00	
11 x 14 two color parchment poster - suitable for framing		
Khaboris Manuscript from Yonan Codex Foundation	20.00	
Selected *Aramaic* translations of New Testament		
Key Thoughts – Collection of the most important thoughts from the *Why...* workshop. *A great daily reminder!*	5.00	
4¼" x 3½" colored cards		
Key Thoughts Screen Saver by Heart Inspired Productions *Check availability*	*20.00	Windows DOS
Pivotal sayings & thoughts used by michael in workshops, tapes & books on 3.5" disk - for PC		
Name That Drag-on by *MindWalks* A computer game based on the Reality Management Worksheet *Check availability*	*30.00	PC MAC
Something has happened. You're *not* happy. Unravel the problem and score points. - 3.5" disk—**state *MAC or PC***		
Hand-crafted Flutes by Coyote Oldman. Beautiful cedar construction. *Played from the heart–easy to learn!*	150.00 / 15.00	165.00
These flutes are used by Coyote Oldman, R. Carlos Nakai and other artists on their recordings. *Priority S&H*		
Carrying Bag for flutes (above) - hand-crafted heavy cloth.	40.00	
Highly recommended for protection and convenience.		
Night Forest by Coyote Oldman - (cassette only)	11.00	
Beautiful music that uses same flute as above.		
Heartland's Favorite Recipes by marijo *Check availability*	*20.00	
Have you heard about the gourmet food at *Heartland?* THIS IS IT!		
HEARTLINES **Why Is This Happening To Me . . . AGAIN?! Newsletter** Published quarterly. One year subscription	18.00	
Health tips for mind, body & spirit, support group information, readers' forum, humor, events schedule, new articles by dr. michael ryce & more.		

Please Enclose Name, Address, Phone, FAX, and E-MAIL	**SUBTOTAL**	
4.00 or 10% of subtotal, whichever is greater to 100.00. Orders 101.00 & above use 5%. *(all foreign orders, please add 20% of Sub Total)*	**SHIPPING and HANDLING**	
Post Office Money Order ONLY To: michael ryce c/o Rt. 3 Box 3280 Theodosia, Missouri 65761	**TOTAL**	

Call or Fax Credit Card Orders:
800-583-9827
(For Credit Card Orders Only Please)

Credit Card # _____

Signature _____ Exp Date _____

Issuing Bank _____ City _____ State _____

Standard bookstore discounts available

HEARTLINES *Newsletter*

Heartlines is a meeting place to communicate on a regular basis with michael and the *Heartland* support team. This newsletter is intended as a tool in developing the skills involved in this work, and as a source of inspiration with which to share insights for aliveness. Support *Heartland's* work *and* keep in touch with one 18.00 purchase per year! This quarterly publication offers an opportunity to stay up-to-date on michael's travel schedule, new articles by michael, *Heartland Intensive and Why Is This Happening To Me . . . AGAIN?!* workshop dates, a listing of support groups around the country, new approaches to working with these tools, and much more.

On the inside you will find *marijo's Selected Recipes*, tips on nutrition and live food, movement and health info, *The Aramaic Connection, In michael's View, More Key Thoughts, Testimonials, Kids' Korner,* and a chance for your input through the *readers' forum.*

You will find subscription information on the *Heartland Products Order Sheet* on pages 200-201.

FLUTES *Hand-crafted In The Native American Tradition by Coyote Oldman*

Consider giving a finely crafted flute to yourself or a friend. They are made of aromatic cedar and have a sweet, melodic sound. Coyote Oldman plays these flutes on his recordings as do many artists including R. Carlos Nakai. They are easy to learn and play. It is not necessary to read music as these flutes are played from the heart and inspire the natural song that exists within each of us. The pure notes that come from these instruments seem to enhance healing and process. Each of these 5 hole flutes, based on the pentatonic scale, is personally voiced and tuned to the key of G by Coyote Oldman. See order sheet on page 201. Please note *Priority S&H* of 15.00.

Forming Support Groups

How can you help?

Help yourself and the extension of this work to every mind on the planet by starting a support group for the study of the *Why Is This Happening To Me . . . AGAIN?!* tools! Support groups provide a safe space to practice and become anchored in the principles taught in this book. They are a place to connect with like-minded people and a place to learn and support each other using these skills. It is not unusual for someone new to this work to have confusion or resistance surface. Being part of a support group provides a space to strengthen yourself by giving and receiving assistance with these tools!

Many support groups begin by showing the video *Why Is This Happening To Me . . . AGAIN?!*, stopping after each hour, and discussing the information presented. One of the most effective ways to learn this work is by teaching and sharing it, another is for group members to rotate in leading the others through a worksheet. It is important to remember to keep the focus on using the tools by doing the Reality management Sheets consistantly.

Heartlines: Why Is This Happening To Me . . . AGAIN?! Newsletter will offer suggestions and tips for forming and continuing support groups. We will also provide an opportunity through our newsletter to help people network with one another for the purpose of connecting with ongoing support groups and forming new ones.

We recommend that at least one member of the group attend a *Heartland* intensive in order to deepen his or her experience with these tools, and share what they have learned.

When we join together in doing our inner work, it accelerates the healing process and provides an opportunity to practice *living* these tools.

Our *Heartland* family joins with you and your family in healing ourselves, each other and the planet.

A Special Notice...

In harmony with our family's commitment to make these tools available to every
mind on the planet, a case of 60 copies of
Why Is This Happening To Me . . . AGAIN?!
can be ordered at 6.00 per book—60% off of
retail—for a total of 360.00 plus 20.00
shipping & handling.

If you have benefited from and wish to
support this work, you might consider giving
books to your friends, selling them wholesale
or retail, and/or donating them to schools,
prisons, orphanages, churches, libraries,
hospitals, halfway houses, drug and alcohol
rehabilitation programs and organizations for
the handi-capable.

Our intention? To share this work...

Lovingly, Gently and with Respect.